e. e. cummings:

a

selection

of

poems

books by e. e. cummings

THE ENORMOUS ROOM (1922)

TULIPS AND CHIMNEYS (1923)

& [AND] (1925)

XLI POEMS (1925)

IS 5 (1926)

HIM (1927)

BY E. E. CUMMINGS (1930)

CIOPW (1931)

W [VIVA] (1931)

EIMI (1933)

NO THANKS (1933)

TOM (1935)

COLLECTED POEMS (1938)

50 POEMS (1940)

I X I (1944)

ANTHROPOS—THE FUTURE OF ART (1945)

SANTA CLAUS (1946)

XAIPE (1950)

I:SIX NONLECTURES (1953)

POEMS: 1923-1954 (1954)

A MISCELLANY (1958)

95 POEMS (1958)

ADVENTURES IN VALUE (*with Marion Morehouse*) (1962)

73 POEMS (1963)

e. e. cummings:
a
selection
of
poems

With an Introduction by
Horace Gregory

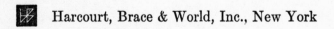 Harcourt, Brace & World, Inc., New York

A Harvest Book

CONTENTS

1 x 1 [one times one] (1944)

1

x

1

XAIPE (1950)

95 poems (1958)

73 poems (1963)

e. e. cummings:

a

selection

of

poems

INTRODUCTION

Before one begins to read the poems in the following pages, it is well to listen to the speaking voice of Edward Estlin Cummings, to overhear his comment on the poems. From these remarks one gathers a few suggestions of how he felt about the writing of them, and of how he wanted his readers to understand their contents. The first passage is from the introduction to his *Collected Poems* of 1938:

The poems to come are for you and for me and are not for mostpeople
—it's no use trying to pretend that mostpeople and ourselves are alike. Mostpeople have less in common with ourselves than the squarerootofminusone. You and I are human beings;mostpeople are snobs.
. . . If mostpeople were to be born twice they'd improbably call it dying—
. . . With you I leave a remembrance of miracles:they are by somebody who can love and who shall be continually reborn. . . .

The second is from *i*, his *six nonlectures*, delivered at Harvard University, 1952-53:

. . . so far as I am concerned, poetry and every other art was and is and forever will be strictly and distinctly a question of individuality . . . poetry is being, not doing. If you wish to follow, even at a distance, the poet's calling (and here, as always, I speak from my own totally biased and entirely personal point of view) you've got to come out of the measurable doing universe into the immeasurable house of being. . . . Nobody else can be alive for you; nor can you be alive for anybody else. Toms can be Dicks and Dicks can be Harrys, but none of them can ever be you.

There's the artist's responsibility; and the most awful responsibility on earth. If you can take it, take it—and be. If you can't, cheer up and go about other people's business; and do (or undo) till you drop.

These conversations faithfully reproduce the rhythms of his voice in prose: one has to read them aloud (or with one's inner ear) to discern the notes of irony, passionate conviction, of courtesy and wit contained within them. As for their meaning, there is a strong Bergsonian twist in their devotion to a philosophy of becoming and rebirth. And what of their trenchant stresses on individuality? That, of course, is part of their aristocratic, elder Americanism—one that has the right to look down on snobs and have nothing whatever to do with them. Throughout the poems, individuality is always respected, and snobbery is always exiled from the shores of Cummings' American Republic.

Cummings was born in a house (not a hospital—a miracle that he did not neglect to mention) in Cambridge, Massachusetts, son of Dr. Edward Cummings, onetime instructor of English, political economy, and sociology for one year each at Harvard, and later minister of the South Congregational Society, Unitarian, of Boston. One almost sees the father's hand on the son's shoulder in Cummings' satires on the condition of man, in their protests against all forms of state tyranny. Cummings' protests revealed the true character of New England Puritan heritage crossed with the emotional temper of St. Francis.

Wherever he walked, wherever he lived, the tradition of his father's independence was sustained, and he was also the most courtly of American poets, a gentleman, one who, as Oscar Wilde would say, "never insults anyone unintentionally." For over thirty years his modest town-house apartment was in Patchin Place, a high-gated, early nineteenth-century cul-de-sac of brick houses facing each other in Greenwich Village in the city of New York. And since his childhood the greater majority of his summers was spent at his family's summer home at Silver Lake, New Hampshire. At both places he guarded his independence and his privacy—and therefore, he and his wife, Marion Morehouse, created an atmosphere in Patchin Place that recalled the distant, pre-bohemian Greenwich Village of Henry James's boyhood memories. The rooms were much-lived in, tiny rooms, made for conversations, and the cheerful welcome, with a handsome silver family teapot on the table and Cummings talking with the same verve and grace and lyrical explosion that enters so much of his prose.

So far we have gathered a few of the beliefs, places, and traditions that enter the contents of the poems in this book. Yet there are other elements that come forward when Cummings speaks of art and "the poet's calling." In this discussion, his position is also that of the artist in a broader sense—in the sense that Marion Morehouse has fine distinction as a photographer, and himself a maker of drawings and paintings—as well as designer of typographical conventions. These conventions are rules, inflexible as laws in playing tennis, brilliantly stressed and pointed, of the way Cummings writes. They are his arrangements of words and parts of words—orderly distortions and punctuations. (There is also a fine light touch of the grammarian in Cummings here.) His employment of the painter's eye in writing brings him into proximity with three twentieth-century French poets: Apollinaire, Henri Michaux, and Jean Cocteau—all of whom, like Cummings, asserted the presence of poetic and visual imagination in multiple forms. There will be a word or two more to say of Cummings' relationship to certain French poets.

We have arrived at the poems themselves, and the more they are reread the more obvious it is that Cummings is one of the greatest lyric poets of all time. From his *six nonlectures* we know something of his learning, his denial of mere knowledge in favor of human wisdom (he was fond of speaking of himself as an "ignoramus"), of his "deep readings" in Dante and Shakespeare during his undergraduate years at Harvard. He knew Chaucer (see "Puella Mea" among his early poems and his sonnet "honour corruption villainy holiness" among his later writings) with memorable awareness; the same was true of his readings in sixteenth- and seventeenth-century lyric poets—particularly in John Wilmot, Earl of Rochester (see "my sweet old etcetera"), and the same quickening discernment attended his readings in the early nineteenth-century Romantics as well as in Dante Gabriel Rossetti and Swinburne. His *six nonlectures* also show something of his familiarity with the Romantic lyricists of France and Germany. To all this he had no pretensions whatsoever: as artist, he may come to warn his readers, but never to teach them—his purpose is to learn, to find his own affinities among unlikely "influences" (see what a magnificent variation of one of Claudel's poems appears in "All in green went my love riding."* How right that poem is in its medieval coloring, for lovers of that time deliberately dressed in green). Two other illustrations of impressions from the French left on Cummings' writings may be noted. One is the poem "in a middle of a room," which recalls, through its imagery, Jean Cocteau's film, *Blood of a Poet*.

> a finger pulls a trigger
> a bird flies into a mirror)

Cummings' entire poem is very like a poem Cocteau may have wished to write, but lacked Cummings' lyric art to do so. Meanwhile the poem has its own being and it compresses within a few lines all that needs to be said of the haunting, drifting impulses toward suicide that had entered twentieth-century consciousness during and after World War I. Among

* In Claudel's *Corona.* "Le sombre Mai."

his other writings, the poem is a tour de force, successfully turned and crisp, yet quite unlike the poems that surround it.

Another tour de force that seems to have been inspired by French poetry is the extraordinary prose poem that closes a series of "Post Impressions" at the end of the "Tulips" section in *Tulips and Chimneys* (1923). The prose poem, or poem in prose, is a French form, best used by Baudelaire, and was an extremely fashionable medium in French writing during the latter years of the nineteenth century. Several American poets (including T. S. Eliot in his "Hysteria") have attempted the form, yet all have fallen short of true accomplishment—except Cummings. In Cummings' poem prose rhythms are fused with dramatic action and they lead—with the greatest economy of words—to the progress of a startling metamorphosis. Only the violence of the transformation saves this "Post Impression" from sentimentality, yet, at the brink of bathos, the poem is saved—and it has the conviction of a daylit nightmare. No less a sign of Cummings' genius in transforming French lyric art into English is his magnificent rendition of Villon's favorite form, the ballade, into a love poem, "a clown's smirk in the skull of a baboon," which is, incidentally, one of the best of poems in English reviving the Pierrot theme handed down to us through survivals of the *commedia dell' arte* on the vaudeville and burlesque stage.

Truly enough, the comic spirit that inspires so many of Cummings' poems has at least one of its sources in the old-fashioned American burlesque show. Only a snob would care to underrate its influence. Certainly, Cummings did not. In the Foreword to *is 5* (1926) he wrote: ". . . my theory of technique, if I have one, is very far from original; nor is it complicated. I can express it in fifteen words, by quoting The Eternal Question And Immortal Answer of burlesk, viz. 'Would you hit a woman with a child?—No, I'd hit her with a brick.' Like the burlesk comedian, I am abnormally fond of that precision which creates movement." His satires and aphoristic verse have the lightness (not without well-timed reports of a burst balloon) of tap-and-soft-shoe dancing. A good case could be made for Cummings as the most refreshing writer of light verse that the twentieth century has known—and this would seem true if this definition of his gift did not lead to underrating his love poems and lyric elegies. No lyric poet of our time has made the love sonnet so clearly and brilliantly his personal instrument as he has—nor in our time has anyone written a devotional sonnet that could be compared with three of his devotional sonnets ("i thank You God for most this amazing," "honor corruption villainy holiness," and the Christmas poem "from spiralling ecstatically this"). No less religious in spirit are his two elegies, first to his mother ("if there are any heavens"), then to his father ("my father moved through dooms of love"). These poems are not only rare and unique in the way that Cummings made them, but rare in the sense that few poets have written memorable poems in tribute to their parents. One must turn back to the eighteenth century, and to William Cowper's lines on "My Mother's Portrait" to find anything that may be compared with them.

One may ask the question: where and how does Cummings' poetry extend the heritage of "the little Athens," New England tradition into our day. From a few of the poems in this selection we know how famously he liked the modern Greeks, and enjoyed their restaurants—but what of the New England tradition itself and his place there? To speculate in this direction, one must not push likenesses and analogies too far, and if one says, "In that tradition, Emily Dickinson was an ancestor," one must also remember that Cummings' poetry is as masculine as hers is feminine, and that—this is important—her poetry exerted no visible influence on his at all. These limitations of the analogy should be kept clear, and once they are, we begin to see how fortunately both poets sustained an aphoristic language they had made their own, a language of sharpened images and verbal wit and action—and mastered with great economy of phrasing. Both poets re-embodied the interweaving lyric themes of life, love, death, and resurrection. So far the analogy holds—and both kept inviolate the transcendental world of their imaginations.

In Cummings' later poems there is increasing richness of imagery drawn from nature, of lyrical variety in his songs and sonnets; the scenes are less urban, and more than a few of the people in the poems live under open skies in a New Hampshire landscape. Even the discovery of a "bespangled clown" in Eighth Street in Greenwich Village seems to have air and light around it, and the increasing absence of a period at the end of poems seems to give the poems more room to breathe, a greater sense of things being alive and growing. It is not too much to say that Cummings in his later poems stressed their flower-like qualities.

And what of the present selection of Cummings' poems? It is for readers who wish to be introduced or reintroduced to some of the best of twentieth-century poetry; it is also proof that lyricism in poetry—something that is more vaguely called "pure poetry" and cannot be described—is as much alive today as it always was. All such poems need is the poet to create them. Cummings was one of those poets: this book contains the evidence. The poems are presented in the chronology of their publication in books. The actual writing of his first three books of poems, *Tulips and Chimneys*, &, and *XLI Poems*, was during the years before and immediately following the publication of his famous World War I novel, *The Enormous Room*, in 1922. These comprised the work of a very young poet, prolific, adventurous, and, at times, dangerously sentimental, particularly in his boyish comments on naked girls in his sonnets. In a number of these the boy in the poem is trying to be a little bit too tough, too hard-boiled, and the nudes are not handsome or intelligent enough to sustain our interest. He wrote far better sonnets— which are included. I have attempted in this chronological order to select poems that transcend the moment of their writing, yet reserving a few of the timely poems to act as pointers through the fabulously glittering 1920's—and the Great Depression (which was anticipated by Cummings' play, *Him*, performed at the Provincetown Playhouse in 1928). His characteristic after-the-event comment is in

> If you can't eat you got to
> smoke and we ain't got
> nothing to smoke: come on kid

The wars of our time are indicated by Cummings' hatred of wars and love of peace. Like the Roman poet Ovid, his commitment and loyalties were to the charms of Venus, not to Mars. Speaking of Ovid, one of his favorite stories, the one about Venus, Mars, and Vulcan, is retold by Cummings in "in heavenly realms of hellas dwelt." As further proof of Cummings' ability to retell a familiar story so that it appears to be completely new—and also to show the poetic vitality of some of his prose—I have chosen a part of his ballet, *Tom*, Episode 2, a description of Eliza of *Uncle Tom's Cabin* crossing the ice. Whatever discriminations, political, moral, or religious, may be found in the poems of Cummings—and this without modifying his convictions or "pulling his punches"—they are transcended by his art. Therefore Cummings had little need to preach. His art is a "seamless garment"; he regarded dullness to be his deepest enemy, and knew himself to be on the side of the angels:

> hear
> ye! the godless are the dull and the dull are the damned

HORACE GREGORY

Palisades,
New York
July 5, 1965

●

Thy fingers make early flowers of
all things.
thy hair mostly the hours love:
a smoothness which
sings, saying
(though love be a day)
do not fear, we will go amaying.

thy whitest feet crisply are straying.
Always
thy moist eyes are at kisses playing,
whose strangeness much
says; singing
(though love be a day)
for which girl art thou flowers bringing?

To be thy lips is a sweet thing
and small.
Death, Thee i call rich beyond wishing
if this thou catch,
else missing.
(though love be a day
and life be nothing, it shall not stop kissing).

All in green went my love riding
on a great horse of gold
into the silver dawn.

four lean hounds crouched low and smiling
the merry deer ran before.

Fleeter be they than dappled dreams
the swift sweet deer
the red rare deer.

Four red roebuck at a white water
the cruel bugle sang before.

Horn at hip went my love riding
riding the echo down
into the silver dawn.

four lean hounds crouched low and smiling
the level meadows ran before.

Softer be they than slippered sleep
the lean lithe deer
the fleet flown deer.

Four fleet does at a gold valley
the famished arrow sang before.

Bow at belt went my love riding
riding the mountain down
into the silver dawn.

four lean hounds crouched low and smiling
the sheer peaks ran before.

Paler be they than daunting death
the sleek slim deer
the tall tense deer.

Four tall stags at a green mountain
the lucky hunter sang before.

All in green went my love riding
on a great horse of gold
into the silver dawn.

four lean hounds crouched low and smiling
my heart fell dead before.

Doll's boy 's asleep
under a stile
he sees eight and twenty
ladies in a line

the first lady
says to nine ladies
his lips drink water
but his heart drinks wine

the tenth lady
says to nine ladies
they must chain his foot
for his wrist 's too fine

the nineteenth
says to nine ladies
you take his mouth
for his eyes are mine.

Doll's boy 's asleep
under the stile
for every mile the feet go
the heart goes nine

when god lets my body be

From each brave eye shall sprout a tree
fruit that dangles therefrom

the purpled world will dance upon
Between my lips which did sing

a rose shall beget the spring
that maidens whom passion wastes

will lay between their little breasts
My strong fingers beneath the snow

Into strenuous birds shall go
my love walking in the grass

their wings will touch with her face
and all the while shall my heart be

With the bulge and nuzzle of the sea

PUELLA MEA

Harun Omar and Master Hafiz
keep your dead beautiful ladies.
Mine is a little lovelier
than any of your ladies were.

In her perfectest array
my lady, moving in the day,
is a little stranger thing
than crisp Sheba with her king
in the morning wandering.
   Through the young and awkward hours
my lady perfectly moving,
through the new world scarce astir
my fragile lady wandering
in whose perishable poise
is the mystery of Spring
(with her beauty more than snow
dexterous and fugitive
my very frail lady drifting
distinctly, moving like a myth
in the uncertain morning, with
April feet like sudden flowers
and all her body filled with May)
—moving in the unskilful day
my lady utterly alive,
to me is a more curious thing
(a thing more nimble and complete)
than ever to Judea's king
were the shapely sharp cunning
and withal delirious feet
of the Princess Salomé

carefully dancing in the noise
of Herod's silence, long ago.

If she a little turn her head
i know that i am wholly dead:
nor ever did on such a throat
the lips of Tristram slowly dote,
La beale Isoud whose leman was.
And if my lady look at me
(with her eyes which like two elves
incredibly amuse themselves)
with a look of færie,
perhaps a little suddenly
(as sometimes the improbable
beauty of my lady will)
—at her glance my spirit shies
rearing (as in the miracle
of a lady who had eyes
which the king's horses might not kill.)
    But should my lady smile, it were
a flower of so pure surprise
(it were so very new a flower,
a flower so frail, a flower so glad)
as trembling used to yield with dew
when the world was young and new
(a flower such as the world had
in Springtime when the world was mad
and Launcelot spoke to Guenever,
a flower which most heavy hung
with silence when the world was young
and Diarmid looked in Grania's eyes.)
    But should my lady's beauty play
at not speaking (sometimes as
it will) the silence of her face

doth immediately make
in my heart so great a noise,
as in the sharp and thirsty blood
of Paris would not all the Troys
of Helen's beauty: never did
Lord Jason (in impossible things
victorious impossibly)
so wholly burn, to undertake
Medea's rescuing eyes; nor he
when swooned the white egyptian day
who with Egypt's body lay.
Lovely as those ladies were
mine is a little lovelier.

And if she speak in her frail way,
it is wholly to bewitch
my smallest thought with a most swift
radiance wherein slowly drift
murmurous things divinely bright;
it is foolingly to smite
my spirit with the lithe free twitch
of scintillant space, with the cool writhe
of gloom truly which syncopate
some sunbeam's skilful fingerings;
it is utterly to lull
with foliate inscrutable
sweetness my soul obedient;
it is to stroke my being with
numbing forests frolicsome,
fleetly mystical, aroam
with keen creatures of idiom
(beings alert and innocent
very deftly upon which
indolent miracles impinge)
—it is distinctly to confute

my reason with the deep caress
of every most shy thing and mute,
it is to quell me with the twinge
of all living intense things.

   Never my soul so fortunate
is (past the luck of all dead men
and loving) as invisibly when
upon her palpable solitude
a furtive occult fragrance steals,
a gesture of immaculate
perfume—whereby (with fear aglow)
my soul is wont wholly to know
the poignant instantaneous fern
whose scrupulous enchanted fronds
toward all things intrinsic yearn,
the immanent subliminal
fern of her delicious voice
(of her voice which always dwells
beside the vivid magical
impetuous and utter ponds
of dream; and very secret food
its leaves inimitable find
beyond the white authentic springs,
beyond the sweet instinctive wells,
which make to flourish the minute
spontaneous meadow of her mind)
—the vocal fern, always which feels
the keen ecstatic actual tread
(and thereto perfectly responds)
of all things exquisite and dead,
all living things and beautiful.

(Caliph and king their ladies had
to love them and to make them glad,
when the world was young and mad,

in the city of Bagdad—
mine is a little lovelier
than any of those ladies were.)

Her body is most beauteous,
being for all things amorous
fashioned very curiously
of roses and of ivory.
The immaculate crisp head
is such as only certain dead
and careful painters love to use
for their youngest angels (whose
praising bodies in a row
between slow glories fleetly go.)
Upon a keen and lovely throat
the strangeness of her face doth float,
which in eyes and lips consists
—always upon the mouth there trysts
curvingly a fragile smile
which like a flower lieth (while
within the eyes is dimly heard
a wistful and precarious bird.)
Springing from fragrant shoulders small,
ardent, and perfectly withal
smooth to stroke and sweet to see
as a supple and young tree,
her slim lascivious arms alight
in skilful wrists which hint at flight
—my lady's very singular
and slenderest hands moreover are
(which as lilies smile and quail)
of all things perfect the most frail.

(Whoso rideth in the tale
of Chaucer knoweth many a pair
of companions blithe and fair;
who to walk with Master Gower
in Confessio doth prefer
shall not lack for beauty there,
nor he that will amaying go
with my lord Boccaccio—
whoso knocketh at the door
of Marie and of Maleore
findeth of ladies goodly store
whose beauty did in nothing err.
If to me there shall appear
than a rose more sweetly known,
more silently than a flower,
my lady naked in her hair—
i for those ladies nothing care
nor any lady dead and gone.)

Each tapering breast is firm and smooth
that in a lovely fashion doth
from my lady's body grow;
as morning may a lily know,
her petaled flesh doth entertain
the adroit blood's mysterious skein
(but like some passionate earlier
flower, the snow will oft utter,
whereof the year has perfect bliss—
for each breast a blossom is,
which being a little while caressed
its fragrance makes the lover blest.)
Her waist is a most tiny hinge
of flesh, a winsome thing and strange;

apt in my hand warmly to lie
it is a throbbing neck whereby
to grasp the belly's ample vase
(that urgent urn which doth amass
for whoso drinks, a dizzier wine
than should the grapes of heaven combine
with earth's madness)—'tis a gate
unto a palace intricate
(whereof the luscious pillars rise
which are her large and shapely thighs)
in whose dome the trembling bliss
of a kingdom wholly is.
    Beneath her thighs such legs are seen
as were the pride of the world's queen:
each is a verb, miraculous
inflected oral devious,
beneath the body's breathing noun
(moreover the delicious frown
of the grave great sensual knees
well might any monarch please.)
Each ankle is divinely shy;
as if for fear you would espy
the little distinct foot (if whose
very minuteness doth abuse
reason, why then the artificer
did most exquisitely err.)

When the world was like a song
heard behind a golden door,
poet and sage and caliph had
to love them and to make them glad
ladies with lithe eyes and long
(when the world was like a flower
Omar Hafiz and Harun
loved their ladies in the moon)

—fashioned very curiously
of roses and of ivory
if naked she appear to me
my flesh is an enchanted tree;
with her lips' most frail parting
my body hears the cry of Spring,
and with their frailest syllable
its leaves go crisp with miracle.

Love!—maker of my lady,
in that always beyond this
poem or any poem she
of whose body words are afraid
perfectly beautiful is,
forgive these words which i have made.
And never boast your dead beauties,
you greatest lovers in the world!
who with Grania strangely fled,
who with Egypt went to bed,
whom white-thighed Semiramis
put up her mouth to wholly kiss—
never boast your dead beauties,
mine being unto me sweeter
(of whose shy delicious glance
things which never more shall be,
perfect things of færie,
are intense inhabitants;
in whose warm superlative
body do distinctly live
all sweet cities passed away—
in her flesh at break of day
are the smells of Nineveh,
in her eyes when day is gone
are the cries of Babylon.)
Diarmid Paris and Solomon,

Omar Harun and Master Hafiz,
to me your ladies are all one—
keep your dead beautiful ladies.

Eater of all things lovely—Time!
upon whose watering lips the world
poises a moment (futile, proud,
a costly morsel of sweet tears)
gesticulates, and disappears—
of all dainties which do crowd
gaily upon oblivion
sweeter than any there is one;
to touch it is the fear of rhyme—
in life's very fragile hour
(when the world was like a tale
made of laughter and of dew,
was a flight, a flower, a flame,
was a tendril fleetly curled
upon frailness) used to stroll
(very slowly) one or two
ladies like flowers made,
softly used to wholly move
slender ladies made of dream
(in the lazy world and new
sweetly used to laugh and love
ladies with crisp eyes and frail,
in the city of Bagdad.)

Keep your dead beautiful ladies
Harun Omar and Master Hafiz.

●

in Just-
spring   when the world is mud-
luscious the little
lame balloonman

whistles   far   and wee

and eddieandbill come
running from marbles and
piracies and it's
spring

when the world is puddle-wonderful

the queer
old balloonman whistles
far   and   wee
and bettyandisbel come dancing

from hop-scotch and jump-rope and

it's
spring
and
     the

          goat-footed

balloonMan   whistles
far
and
wee

●

Tumbling-hair
    picker of buttercups
       violets

dandelions
And the big bullying daisies
       through the field wonderful
with eyes a little sorry
Another comes
    also picking flowers

●
1.

the emperor
sleeps in a palace of porphyry
which was a million years building
he takes the air in a howdah
of jasper beneath saffron
umbrellas
upon an elephant
twelve feet high
behind whose ear
sits always a crowned
king twir-
ling an
ankus of
ebony
the fountains of the emperor's
palace run sunlight and
moonlight and the emperor's
elephant is a thousand years old

the harem of
the emperor
is carpeted with
gold cloth
from the
ceiling (one
diamond timid
with nesting incense)
fifty
marble
pillars
slipped from immeasurable
height, fall, fifty, silent

in the incense is tangled a cool moon
there are thrice-three-hundred
doors carven of chalcedony and
before every door a naked
eunuch watches
on their heads turbans of a hundred
colours
in their hands scimitars like windy torches
each
is
blacker than oblivion

the ladies
of the emperor's
harem are queens
of all the earth and the rings
upon their hands are from mines
a mile deep
but the body of
the queen of queens is
more transparent
than water, she is softer than birds

2.

when the emperor is very
amorous he reclines upon
the couch of couches and
beckons   with
the little
finger of his left
hand
      then the
thrice-three-hundredth

door is opened by the tallest
eunuch and the queen
of queens comes
forth
ankles
musical with large pearls
kingdoms in her ears
at the feet of
the emperor a cithern-
player squats with
quiveringgold
body
behind
the emperor ten
elected warriors with
bodies of lazy jade
and twitching
eyelids
finger
their
unquiet
spears

the queen of queens is dancing

her subtle
body weaving
insinuating upon the gold cloth
incessantly creates patterns of sudden
lust
her
stealing body ex-
pending gathering pouring upon itself   stiffenS
to a
white thorn
of desire

the taut neck of the citharede wags
in the dust the ghastly warriors
amber with lust breathe
together   the emperor, exerting
himself among his pillows throws
jewels at the queen of queens and
white money upon her nakedness
he
nods
          and all
depart through the bruised air aflutter with pearls

3.

they are
alone
he beckons, she rises she
stands
a moment
in the passion of the fifty
pillars
listening

while the queens of all the
earth writhe upon deep rugs

your little voice
                  Over the wires came leaping
and i felt suddenly
dizzy
       With the jostling and shouting of merry flowers
wee skipping high-heeled flames
courtesied before my eyes
                      or twinkling over to my side
Looked up
with impertinently exquisite faces
floating hands were laid upon me
I was whirled and tossed into delicious dancing
up
Up
with the pale important
                  stars and the Humorous
                            moon
dear girl
How i was crazy how i cried when i heard
                    over time
and tide and death
leaping
Sweetly
       your voice

●

LA GUERRE

I

the bigness of cannon
is skilful,

but i have seen
death's clever enormous voice
which hides in a fragility
of poppies . . . .

i say that sometimes
on these long talkative animals
are laid fists of huger silence.

I have seen all the silence
filled with vivid noiseless boys

at Roupy
i have seen
between barrages,

the night utter ripe unspeaking girls.

II

O sweet spontaneous
earth how often have
the
doting

        fingers of
prurient philosophers pinched

and
poked

thee
, has the naughty thumb
of science prodded
thy

    beauty   . how
often have religions taken
thee upon their scraggy knees
squeezing and

buffeting thee that thou mightest conceive
gods
    (but
true

to the incomparable
couch of death thy
rhythmic
lover

    thou answerest

them only with

      spring)

Buffalo Bill 's
defunct
          who used to
          ride a watersmooth-silver
                              stallion
and break onetwothreefourfive pigeonsjustlikethat
                                        Jesus

he was a handsome man
                    and what i want to know is
how do you like your blueeyed boy
Mister Death

at the head of this street a gasping organ is waving motheaten tunes.   a fatish hand turns the crank; the box sprouts
fairies, out of it sour gnomes tumble clumsily, the little box
is spilling rancid elves upon neat sunlight into the flowerstricken air which is filthy with agile swarming sonal creatures

—Children, stand with circular frightened faces glaring at
the shabby tiny smiling, man in whose hand the crank goes
desperately, round and round pointing to the queer monkey

(if you toss him a coin he will pick it cleverly from, the air
and stuff it seriously in, his minute pocket) Sometimes he
does not catch a piece of money and then his master will
yell at him over the music and jerk the little string and the
monkey will sit, up, and look at, you with his solemn blinky
eyeswhichneversmile and after he has caught a, penny or
three, pennies he will be thrown a peanut (which he will
open skilfully with his, mouth carefully holding, it, in his
little toylike hand) and then he will stiff-ly throw the shell
away with a small bored gesture that makes the children
laugh.

But i don't, the crank goes round desperate elves and hopeless gnomes and frantic fairies gush clumsily from the
battered box fatish and mysterious the flowerstricken sunlight is thickening dizzily is reeling gently the street and
the children and the monkeyandtheorgan and the man are
dancing slowly are tottering up and down in a trembly mist
of atrocious melody . . . . tiniest dead tunes crawl upon my
face my hair is lousy with mutilated singing microscopic
things in my ears scramble faintly tickling putrescent
atomies,

and

i feel the jerk of the little string! the tiny smiling shabby man is yelling over the music i understand him i shove my round red hat back on my head i sit up and blink at you with my solemn eyeswhichneversmile

yes, By god.
for i am they are pointing at the queer monkey with a little oldish doll-like face and hairy arms like an ogre and rubbercoloured hands and feet filled with quick fingers and a remarkable tail which is allbyitself alive. (and he has a little red coat with i have a real pocket in it and the round funny hat with a big feather is tied under myhis chin.) that climbs and cries and runs and floats like a toy on the end of a string

ladies and gentlemen this little girl
with the good teeth and small important breasts
(is it the Frolic or the Century whirl?
one's memory indignantly protests)
this little dancer with the tightened eyes
crisp ogling shoulders and the ripe quite too
large lips always clenched faintly, wishes you
with all her fragile might to not surmise
she dreamed one afternoon

                 . . . . or maybe read?

of a time when the beautiful most of her
(this here and This, do you get me?)
will maybe dance and maybe sing and be
absitively posolutely dead,
like Coney Island in winter

it may not always be so; and i say
that if your lips, which i have loved, should touch
another's, and your dear strong fingers clutch
his heart, as mine in time not far away;
if on another's face your sweet hair lay
in such a silence as i know, or such
great writhing words as, uttering overmuch
stand helplessly before the spirit at bay;

if this should be, i say if this should be—
you of my heart, send me a little word;
that i may go unto him, and take his hands,
saying, Accept all happiness from me.
Then shall i turn my face, and hear one bird
sing terribly afar in the lost lands.

a wind has blown the rain away and blown
the sky away and all the leaves away,
and the trees stand.   I think i too have known
autumn too long

                    (and what have you to say,
wind wind wind—did you love somebody
and have you the petal of somewhere in your heart
pinched from dumb summer?
                              O crazy daddy
of death dance cruelly for us and start

the last leaf whirling in the final brain
of air!) Let us as we have seen see
doom's integration . . . . a wind has blown the rain

away and the leaves and the sky and the
trees stand:
              the trees stand.   The trees,
suddenly wait against the moon's face.

by little accurate saints thickly which tread
the serene nervous light of paradise—
by angelfaces clustered like bright lice

about god's capable dull important head—
by on whom glories whisperingly impinge
(god's pretty mother)but may not confuse

the clever hair nor rout the young mouth whose
lips begin a smile exactly strange—
this painter should have loved my lady.
And by this throat a little suddenly lifted

in singing—hands fragile whom almost tire
the sleepshaped lilies—

                    should my lady's body
with these frail ladies dangerously respire:

impeccable girls in raiment laughter-gifted.

notice the convulsed orange inch of moon
perching on this silver minute of evening.

We'll choose the way to the forest—no offense
to you, white town whose spires softly dare.
Will take the houseless wisping rune
of road lazily carved on sharpening air.

Fields lying miraculous in violent silence

fill with microscopic whithering
. . .(that's the Black People, chérie,
who live under stones.) Don't be afraid

and we will pass the simple ugliness
of exact tombs, where a large road crosses
and all the people are minutely dead.

Then you will slowly kiss me

●

the wind is a Lady with
bright slender eyes(who

moves)at sunset
and who—touches—the
hills without any reason

(i have spoken with this
indubitable and green person "Are
You the wind?" "Yes" "why do you touch flowers
as if they were unalive, as

if They were ideas?" "because, sir
things which in my mind blossom will
stumble beneath a clumsiest disguise, appear
capable of fragility and indecision

—do not suppose these
without any reason and otherwise
roses and mountains
different from the i am who wanders

imminently across the renewed world"
to me said the)wind being A lady in a green
dress, who; touches: the fields
(at sunset)

Take for example this:

if to the colour of midnight
to a more than darkness(which
is myself and Paris and all
things)the bright
rain
occurs deeply, beautifully

and i(being at a window
in this midnight)
                    for no reason feel
deeply completely conscious of the rain or rather
Somebody who uses roofs and streets skilfully to make a
possible and beautiful sound:

if a(perhaps)clock strikes, in the alive
coolness, very faintly and
finally through altogether delicate gestures of rain

a colour comes, which is morning, O do not wonder that

(just at the edge of day)i surely
make a millionth poem which will not wholly
miss you; or if i certainly create, lady,
one of the thousand selves who are your smile.

●

Paris; this April sunset completely utters
utters serenely silently a cathedral
before whose upward lean magnificent face
the streets turn young with rain,

spiral acres of bloated rose
coiled within cobalt miles of sky
yield to and heed
the mauve
        of twilight(who slenderly descends,
daintily carrying in her eyes the dangerous first stars)
people move love hurry in a gently

arriving gloom and
see!(the new moon
fills abruptly with sudden silver
these torn pockets of lame and begging colour)while
there and here the lithe indolent prostitute
Night, argues

with certain houses

suppose
Life is an old man carrying flowers on his head.

young death sits in a café
smiling, a piece of money held between
his thumb and first finger

(i say "will he buy flowers" to you
and "Death is young
life wears velour trousers
life totters, life has a beard" i

say to you who are silent.—"Do you see
Life? he is there and here,
or that, or this
or nothing or an old man 3 thirds
asleep, on his head
flowers, always crying
to nobody something about les
roses les bluets
                    yes,
                        will He buy?
Les belles bottes—oh hear
, pas chères")

and my love slowly answered I think so.   But
I think I see someone else

there is a lady, whose name is Afterwards
she is sitting beside young death, is slender;
likes flowers.

●

here is little Effie's head
whose brains are made of gingerbread
when the judgment day comes
God will find six crumbs

stooping by the coffinlid
waiting for something to rise
as the other somethings did—
you imagine His surprise

bellowing through the general noise
Where is Effie who was dead?
—to God in a tiny voice,
i am may the first crumb said

whereupon its fellow five
crumbs chuckled as if they were alive
and number two took up the song,
might i'm called and did no wrong

cried the third crumb, i am should
and this is my little sister could
with our big brother who is would
don't punish us for we were good;

and the last crumb with some shame
whispered unto God, my name
is must and with the others i've
been Effie who isn't alive

just imagine it I say
God amid a monstrous din
watch your step and follow me
stooping by Effie's little, in

(want a match or can you see?)
which the six subjunctive crumbs
twitch like mutilated thumbs:
picture His peering biggest whey

coloured face on which a frown
puzzles, but I know the way—
(nervously Whose eyes approve
the blessed while His ears are crammed

with the strenuous music of
the innumerable capering damned)
—staring wildly up and down
the here we are now judgment day

cross the threshold have no dread
lift the sheet back in this way.
here is little Effie's head
whose brains are made of gingerbread

•

Who
        threw the silver dollar up into the tree?

                                    I didn't
said the little lady who sews and grows every day
paler-paler she sits sewing and growing and that's the
truth,
who threw

            the ripe melon into the tree?you
                                    got me
said the smoke who runs the elevator but I bet two bits
come seven come eleven m m make the world safe for
democracy it never fails and that's a fact;

who threw the

bunch of violets
                    into the tree?I dunno said the silver
dog,   with ripe eyes and wagged his tail that's the
god's own

and the moon kissed the little lady on her paler-paler
face and said never mind,you'll find
                                    But the moon
creeped into the pink hand of the smoke that shook
the ivories
                and she said said She Win and you won't
be sorry   And The Moon came!along-along to the
waggy silver dog
and the moon came
and the Moon said into his Ripe Eyes
                                    and the moon
  Smiled
  , so

●

my girl's tall with hard long eyes
as she stands, with her long hard hands keeping
silence on her dress, good for sleeping
is her long hard body filled with surprise
like a white shocking wire, when she smiles
a hard long smile it sometimes makes
gaily go clean through me tickling aches,
and the weak noise of her eyes easily files
my impatience to an edge—my girl's tall
and taut, with thin legs just like a vine
that's spent all of its life on a garden-wall,
and is going to die.   When we grimly go to bed
with these legs she begins to heave and twine
about me, and to kiss my face and head.

●

i like my body when it is with your
body.   It is so quite new a thing.
Muscles better and nerves more.
i like your body.   i like what it does,
i like its hows.   i like to feel the spine
of your body and its bones, and the trembling
-firm-smooth ness and which i will
again and again and again
kiss,   i like kissing this and that of you,
i like, slowly stroking the, shocking fuzz
of your electric fur, and what-is-it comes
over parting flesh . . . . And eyes big love-crumbs,

and possibly i like the thrill

of under me you so quite new

•

little tree
little silent Christmas tree
you are so little
you are more like a flower

who found you in the green forest
and were you very sorry to come away?
see   i will comfort you
because you smell so sweetly

i will kiss your cool bark
and hug you safe and tight
just as your mother would,
only don't be afraid

look   the spangles
that sleep all the year in a dark box
dreaming of being taken out and allowed to shine,
the balls the chains red and gold the fluffy threads,

put up your little arms
and i'll give them all to you to hold
every finger shall have its ring
and there won't be a single place dark or unhappy

then when you're quite dressed
you'll stand in the window for everyone to see
and how they'll stare!
oh but you'll be very proud

and my little sister and i will take hands
and looking up at our beautiful tree
we'll dance and sing
"Noel Noel"

●

one April dusk the
sallow street-lamps were turning
snowy against a west of robin's egg blue when
i entered a mad street whose

mouth dripped with slavver of
spring
chased two flights of squirrel-stairs into
a mid-victorian attic which is known as
Ο ΠΑΡΘΕΝΩΝ
                    and having ordered
yaoorti from
Nicho'
settled my feet on the

ceiling inhaling six divine inches
of Haremina   in
the thick of the snick-
er of cards and smack of back-

gammon boards i was aware of an entirely
dirty circle of habitues their
faces like cigarettebutts, chewed
with disdain,   lead by a Jumpy

Tramp who played each
card as if it were a thunderbolt red-
hot   peeling
off huge slabs of a fuzzy

language with the aid of an exclamatory
tooth-pick
And who may that
be i said exhaling into

eternity as Nicho' laid
before me bread
more downy than street-lamps
upon an almostclean

plate
"Achilles"
said
Nicho'

"and did you perhaps wish also shishkabob?"

●

the skinny voice

of the leatherfaced
woman with the crimson
nose and coquettishly-
cocked bonnet

having ceased   the

captain
announces that as three
dimes seven nickels and ten
pennies have been deposited upon

the drum   there is need

of just twenty five cents
dear friends
to make it an even
dollar   whereupon

the Divine Average who was

attracted by the inspired
sister's howling moves
off
will anyone tell him why he should

blow two bits for the coming of Christ Jesus

?
??
???
!

nix, kid

it's just like a coffin's
inside when you die,
pretentious and
shiny and
not too wide
　　　　　dear god

there's a portrait
over the door very notable of
the sultan's nose pullable and rosy
flanked by the scrumptious magdalene
of whoisit and madame
something by gainsborough
　　　　　　　　　just the playthings
　　　　　　　　　for dust　n'est-ce pas

　effendi drifts between
　tables like an old leaf
　between toadstools
he is the cheerfulest of men
　his peaked head smoulders
　like a new turd in April
　his legs are brittle and small
　his feet large and fragile
his queer hands twitter before him, like foolish
　butterflies
he is the most courteous of men

should you remark the walls have been repapered

he will nod
　　　　　like buddha
　　　　　or answer modestly
i am dying

so let us come in together and
drink coffee covered with froth
half-mud
and not too
sweet?

●

5
derbies-with-men-in-them smoke Helmar
cigarettes   2
play backgammon, 3 watch

a has gold
teeth b pink
suspenders c
reads Atlantis

x and y play   b
cries "effendi" "Uh" "coffee"
"uh"   enter
paperboy, c

buys Bawstinamereekin, exit
paperboy   a finishes
Helmar   lights
another

        x and y
play, effendi approaches, sets
down coffee   withdraws
a and c discuss news in

turkish x and y play b spits
x and
y
play, b starts armenian record

                              pho
nographisrunn
ingd o   w, n   phonograph
                   stopS.

b swears in persian at phonograph
x wins   exeunt ax: by; c,
Goo dnightef fendi
. . . .

five men in derbies

●

O Thou to whom the musical white spring

offers her lily inextinguishable,
taught by thy tremulous grace bravely to fling

Implacable death's mysteriously sable
robe from her redolent shoulders,
                              Thou from whose
feet reincarnate song suddenly leaping
flameflung, mounts, inimitably to lose
herself where the wet stars softly are keeping

their exquisite dreams—O Love! upon thy dim
shrine of intangible commemoration,
(from whose faint close as some grave languorous hymn

pledged to illimitable dissipation
unhurried clouds of incense fleetly roll)

i spill my bright incalculable soul.

this is the garden: colours come and go,
frail azures fluttering from night's outer wing
strong silent greens serenely lingering,
absolute lights like baths of golden snow.
This is the garden: pursed lips do blow
upon cool flutes within wide glooms, and sing
(of harps celestial to the quivering string)
invisible faces hauntingly and slow.

This is the garden.   Time shall surely reap
and on Death's blade lie many a flower curled,
in other lands where other songs be sung;
yet stand They here enraptured, as among
the slow deep trees perpetual of sleep
some silver-fingered fountain steals the world.

I have seen her a stealthily frail
flower walking with its fellows in the death
of light, against whose enormous curve of flesh
exactly cubes of tiny fragrance try;
i have watched certain petals rapidly wish
in the corners of her youth; whom, fiercely shy
and gently brutal, the prettiest wrath
of blossoms dishevelling made a pale
fracas upon the accurate moon . . . .
Across the important gardens her body
will come toward me with its hurting sexual smell
of lilies . . . . beyond night's silken immense swoon
the moon is like a floating silver hell
a song of adolescent ivory.

●

who's most afraid of death? thou
                                    art of him
utterly afraid, i love of thee
(beloved) this

                    and truly i would be
near when his scythe takes crisply the whim
of thy smoothness.   and mark the fainting
murdered petals.   with the caving stem.

But of all most would i be one of them

round the hurt heart which do so frailly cling . . . .)
i who am but imperfect in my fear

Or with thy mind against my mind, to hear
nearing our hearts' irrevocable play—
through the mysterious high futile day

an enormous stride
                        (and drawing thy mouth toward

my mouth, steer our lost bodies carefully downward)

Jimmie's got a goil
                    goil
                         goil,
                              Jimmie
's got a goil and
she coitnly can shimmie

when you see her shake
                       shake
                            shake,
                                  when
you see her shake a
shimmie how you wish that you was Jimmie.

Oh for such a gurl
                   gurl
                        gurl,
                             oh
for such a gurl to
be a fellow's twistandtwirl

talk about your Sal-
                    Sal-
                        Sal-,
                             talk
about your Salo
-mes but gimmie Jimmie's gal.

listen my children and you
shall hear the true

story of Mr Do
-nothing the wellknown parvenu
who

(having dreamed of a corkscrew)
studied with Freud a year or two
and when Freud got through
with Do-

nothing Do
-nothing could do
nothing which you
and i are accustomed to
accomplish two

or three times, and even a few
more depending on the remu-
nerativeness of the stimulus(eheu
fu
-gaces Postu-
me boo

who)

even if all desires things moments be
murdered known photographed,ourselves yawning will ask
    ourselves
où sont les neiges. . . . some

guys talks big

about Lundun Burlin an gay Paree an
some guys claims der never was
nutn like Nooer Leans Shikahgo Sain
Looey Noo York an San Fran dictaphones
wireless subways vacuum
cleaners pianolas funnygraphs skyscrapers an safetyrazors

sall right in its way kiddo
but as fer i gimme de good ole daze. . . .

in dem daze kid Christmas
meant sumpn youse knows wot
i refers ter Satter Nailyuh(comes but once er
year)i'll tell de woild one swell bangup
time wen nobody wore no cloze
an went runnin aroun wid eachudder Hell
Bent fer election makin believe dey was chust born

it really must
be Nice, never to

have no imagination)or never
never to wonder about guys you used to(and them
slim hot queens with dam next to nothing

on)tangoing
(while a feller tries
to hold down the fifty bucks per
job with one foot and rock a

cradle with the other)it Must be
nice never to have no doubts about why you
put the ring
on(and watching her
face grow old and tired to which

you're married and hands get red washing
things and dishes)and to never, never really wonder i
mean about the smell
of babies and how you

know the dam rent's going to and everything and never,
  never
Never to stand at no window
because i can't sleep(smoking sawdust

cigarettes in the
middle of the night

•

mr youse needn't be so spry
concernin questions arty

each has his tastes but as for i
i likes a certain party

gimme the he-man's solid bliss
for youse ideas i'll match youse

a pretty girl who naked is
is worth a million statues

than(by yon sunset's wintry glow
revealed)this tall strong stalwart youth,
what sight shall human optics know
more quite ennobling forsooth?

One wondrous fine sonofabitch
(to all purposes and intents)
in which distinct and rich
portrait should be included,gents

these(by the fire's ruddy glow
united)not less than sixteen
children and of course you know
their mother,of his heart the queen

—incalculable bliss!
Picture it gents:our hero,Dan
who as you've guessed already is
the poorbuthonest workingman

(by that bright flame whose myriad tints
enrich a visage simple,terse,
seated like any king or prince
upon his uncorrupted arse

with all his hearty soul aglow)
his nightly supper sups
it isn't snowing snow you know
it's snowing buttercups

MEMORABILIA

stop look &

listen Venezia: incline thine
ear you glassworks
of Murano;
pause
elevator nel
mezzo del cammin' that means half-
way up the Campanile, believe

thou me cocodrillo—

mine eyes have seen
the glory of

the coming of
the Americans particularly the
brand of marriageable nymph which is
armed with large legs rancid
voices Baedekers Mothers and kodaks
—by night upon the Riva Schiavoni or in
the felicitous vicinity of the de l'Europe

Grand and Royal
Danielli their numbers

are like unto the stars of Heaven. . . .

i do signore
affirm that all gondola signore
day below me gondola signore gondola
and above me pass loudly and gondola
rapidly denizens of Omaha Altoona or what
not enthusiastic cohorts from Duluth God only,
gondola knows Cincingondolanati i gondola don't

—the substantial dollarbringing virgins
"from the Loggia where
are we angels by O yes
beautiful we now pass through the look
girls in the style of that's the
foliage what is it didn't Ruskin
says about you got the haven't Marjorie
isn't this wellcurb simply darling"
                              —O Education:O

thos cook & son

(O to be a metope
now that triglyph's here)

●

(ponder,darling,these busted statues
of yon motheaten forum be aware
notice what hath remained
—the stone cringes
clinging to the stone,how obsolete

lips utter their extant smile . . . .
remark

a few deleted of texture
or meaning monuments and dolls

resist Them Greediest Paws of careful
time all of which is extremely
unimportant)whereas Life

matters if or

when the your- and my-
idle vertical worthless
self unite in a peculiarly
momentary

partnership(to instigate
constructive
                Horizontal
business . . . . even so,let us make haste
—consider well this ruined aqueduct

lady,
which used to lead something into somewhere)

"next to of course god america i
love you land of the pilgrims' and so forth oh
say can you see by the dawn's early my
country 'tis of centuries come and go
and are no more what of it we should worry
in every language even deafanddumb
thy sons acclaim your glorious name by gorry
by jingo by gee by gosh by gum
why talk of beauty what could be more beautiful than these heroic happy dead
who rushed like lions to the roaring slaughter
they did not stop to think they died instead
then shall the voice of liberty be mute?"

He spoke.   And drank rapidly a glass of water

look at this)
a 75 done
this nobody would
have believed
would they no
kidding this was my particular

pal
funny aint
it we was
buddies
i used to

know
him lift the
poor cuss
tenderly this side up **handle**

with care
fragile
and send him home

to his old mother in
a new nice pine box

(collect

come, gaze with me upon this dome
of many coloured glass, and see
his mother's pride, his father's joy,
unto whom duty whispers low

"thou must!" and who replies "I can!"
—yon clean upstanding well dressed boy
that with his peers full oft hath quaffed
the wine of life and found it sweet—

a tear within his stern blue eye,
upon his firm white lips a smile,
one thought alone: to do or die
for God for country and for Yale

above his blond determined head
the sacred flag of truth unfurled,
in the bright heyday of his youth
the upper class American

unsullied stands, before the world:
with manly heart and conscience free,
upon the front steps of her home
by the high minded pure young girl

much kissed, by loving relatives
well fed, and fully photographed
the son of man goes forth to war
with trumpets clap and syphilis

●

my sweet old etcetera
aunt lucy during the recent

war could and what
is more did tell you just
what everybody was fighting

for,
my sister

isabel created hundreds
(and
hundreds)of socks not to
mention shirts fleaproof earwarmers

etcetera wristers etcetera, my
mother hoped that

i would die etcetera
bravely of course my father used
to become hoarse talking about how it was
a privilege and if only he
could meanwhile my

self etcetera lay quietly
in the deep mud et

cetera
(dreaming,
et
     cetera, of
Your smile
eyes knees and of your Etcetera)

since feeling is first
who pays any attention
to the syntax of things
will never wholly kiss you;

wholly to be a fool
while Spring is in the world

my blood approves,
and kisses are a better fate
than wisdom
lady i swear by all flowers.   Don't cry
—the best gesture of my brain is less than
your eyelids' flutter which says

we are for each other: then
laugh, leaning back in my arms
for life's not a paragraph

And death i think is no parenthesis

after all white horses are in bed

will you walking beside me, my very lady,
if scarcely the somewhat city
wiggles in considerable twilight

touch (now) with a suddenly unsaid

gesture lightly my eyes?
And send life out of me and the night
absolutely into me. . . . a wise
and puerile moving of your arm will
do suddenly that

                    will do
more than heroes beautifully in shrill
armour colliding on huge blue horses,
and the poets looked at them, and made verses,

through the sharp light cryingly as the knights flew.

touching you i say (it being Spring
and night) "let us go a very little beyond
the last road—there's something to be found"

and smiling you answer "everything
turns into something else, and slips away. . . .
(these leaves are Thingish with moondrool
and i'm ever so very little afraid")
                                        i say
"along this particular road the moon if you'll
notice follows us like a big yellow dog.   You

don't believe? look back. (Along the sand
behind us, a big yellow dog that's . . . . now it's red
a big red dog that may be owned by who
knows)
            only turn a little your. so. And

there's the moon, there is something faithful and mad"

along the brittle treacherous bright streets
of memory comes my heart,singing like
an idiot,whispering like a drunken man

who(at a certain corner,suddenly)meets
the tall policeman of my mind.
                              awake
being not asleep,elsewhere our dreams began
which now are folded:but the year completes
his life as a forgotten prisoner

—"Ici?"—"Ah non, mon chéri; il fait trop froid"—
they are gone:along these gardens moves a wind bringing
rain and leaves,filling the air with fear
and sweetness . . . . pauses.   (Halfwhispering . . . . half-
    singing

stirs the always smiling chevaux de bois)

when you were in Paris we met here

if i have made,my lady,intricate
imperfect various things chiefly which wrong
your eyes(frailer than most deep dreams are frail)
songs less firm than your body's whitest song
upon my mind—if i have failed to snare
the glance too shy—if through my singing slips
the very skillful strangeness of your smile
the keen primeval silence of your hair

—let the world say "his most wise music stole
nothing from death"—
                    you only will create
(who are so perfectly alive)my shame:
lady through whose profound and fragile lips
the sweet small clumsy feet of April came

into the ragged meadow of my soul.

Space being(don't forget to remember)Curved
(and that reminds me who said o yes Frost
Something there is which isn't fond of walls)

an electromagnetic(now I've lost
the)Einstein expanded Newton's law preserved
conTinuum(but we read that beFore)

of Course life being just a Reflex you
know since Everything is Relative or

to sum it All Up god being Dead(not to

mention inTerred)
     LONG LIVE that Upwardlooking
Serene Illustrious and Beatific
Lord of Creation,MAN:
      at a least crooking
of Whose compassionate digit,earth's most terrific

quadruped swoons into billiardBalls!

●

remarked Robinson Jefferson

to Injustice Taughed
your story is so interested

but you make me laft
welates Wouldwoe Washington
to Lydia E. McKinley

when Buch tooked out his C.O.D.
Abe tucks it up back inley
clamored Clever Rusefelt
to Theodore Odysseus Graren't

we couldn't free the negro
because he ant
but Coolitch wiped his valley forge

with Sitting Bull's T.P.
and the duckbilled platitude lays & lays

and Lays aytash unee

the first president to be loved by his
bitterest enemies" is dead

the only man woman or child who wrote
a simple declarative sentence with seven grammatical
errors "is dead"
beautiful Warren Gamaliel Harding
"is" dead
he's
"dead"
if he wouldn't have eaten them Yapanese Craps

somebody might hardly never not have been
                    unsorry,perhaps

●

in a middle of a room
stands a suicide
sniffing a Paper rose
smiling to a self

"somewhere it is Spring and sometimes
people are in real:imagine
somewhere real flowers,but
I can't imagine real flowers for if I

could,they would somehow
not Be real"
(so he smiles
smiling)"but I will not

everywhere be real to
you in a moment"
The is blond
with small hands

"& everything is easier
than I had guessed everything would
be;even remembering the way who
looked at whom first,anyhow dancing"

(a moon swims out of a cloud
a clock strikes midnight
a finger pulls a trigger
a bird flies into a mirror)

if there are any heavens my mother will(all by herself)have
one.   It will not be a pansy heaven nor
a fragile heaven of lilies-of-the-valley but
it will be a heaven of blackred roses

my father will be(deep like a rose
tall like a rose)

standing near my

(swaying over her
silent)
with eyes which are really petals and see

nothing with the face of a poet really which
is a flower and not a face with
hands
which whisper
This is my beloved my

                    (suddenly in sunlight
he will bow,

& the whole garden will bow)

a clown's smirk in the skull of a baboon
(where once good lips stalked or eyes firmly stirred)
my mirror gives me,on this afternoon;
i am a shape that can but eat and turd
ere with the dirt death shall him vastly gird,
a coward waiting clumsily to cease
whom every perfect thing meanwhile doth miss;
a hand's impression in an empty glove,
a soon forgotten tune,a house for lease.
I have never loved you dear as now i love

behold this fool who,in the month of June,
having of certain stars and planets heard,
rose very slowly in a tight balloon
until the smallening world became absurd;
him did an archer spy(whose aim had erred
never)and by that little trick or this
he shot the aeronaut down,into the abyss
—and wonderfully i fell through the green groove
of twilight,striking into many a piece.
I have never loved you dear as now i love

god's terrible face,brighter than a spoon,
collects the image of one fatal word;
so that my life(which liked the sun and the moon)
resembles something that has not occurred:
i am a birdcage without any bird,
a collar looking for a dog,a kiss
without lips;a prayer lacking any knees
but something beats within my shirt to prove
he is undead who,living,noone is.
I have never loved you dear as now i love.

Hell(by most humble me which shall increase)
open thy fire! for i have had some bliss
of one small lady upon earth above;
to whom i cry,remembering her face,
i have never loved you dear as now i love

somewhere i have never travelled,gladly beyond
any experience,your eyes have their silence:
in your most frail gesture are things which enclose me,
or which i cannot touch because they are too near

your slightest look easily will unclose me
though i have closed myself as fingers,
you open always petal by petal myself as Spring opens
(touching skilfully,mysteriously)her first rose

or if your wish be to close me,i and
my life will shut very beautifully,suddenly,
as when the heart of this flower imagines
the snow carefully everywhere descending;

nothing which we are to perceive in this world equals
the power of your intense fragility:whose texture
compels me with the colour of its countries,
rendering death and forever with each breathing

(i do not know what it is about you that closes
and opens;only something in me understands
the voice of your eyes is deeper than all roses)
nobody,not even the rain,has such small hands

is there a flower(whom
i meet anywhere
able to be and seem
so quite softly as your hair

what bird has perfect fear
(of suddenly me)like these
first deepest rare
quite who are your eyes

(shall any dream
come a more millionth mile
shyly to its doom
than you will smile)

●

my darling since
you and
i are thoroughly haunted by
what neither is any
echo of dream nor
any flowering of any

echo(but the echo
of the flower of

Dreaming)somewhere behind us
always trying(or sometimes trying under
us)to is it
find somehow(but O gracefully)a
we,entirely whose least

breathing may surprise
ourselves
       —let's then
despise what is not courage my

darling(for only Nobody knows
where truth grows why
birds fly and
especially who the moon is.

●

nothing is more exactly terrible than
to be alone in the house,with somebody and
with something)
                    You are gone.   there is laughter

and despair impersonates a street

i lean from the window,behold ghosts,
                                    a man
hugging a woman in a park.   Complete.

and slightly(why?or lest we understand)
slightly i am hearing somebody
coming up stairs,carefully
(carefully climbing carpeted flight after
carpeted flight.   in stillness,climbing
the carpeted stairs of terror)

and continually i am seeing something

inhaling gently a cigarette(in a mirror

put off your faces,Death:for day is over
(and such a day as must remember he
who watched unhands describe what mimicry,

with angry seasalt and indignant clover
marrying to themselves Life's animals)

but not darkness shall quite outmarch forever
—and i perceive,within transparent walls
how several smoothly gesturing stars are clever
to persuade even silence:therefore wonder

opens a gate;the prisoner dawn embraces

hugely some few most rare perfectly dear
(and worlds whirl beyond worlds:immortal yonder
collidingly absorbs eternal near)

day being come,Love,put on your faces

but if a living dance upon dead minds
why,it is love;but at the earliest spear
of sun perfectly should disappear
moon's utmost magic,or stones speak or one
name control more incredible splendor than
our merely universe,love's also there:
and being here imprisoned,tortured here
love everywhere exploding maims and blinds
(but surely does not forget,perish,sleep
cannot be photographed,measured;disdains
the trivial labelling of punctual brains. . .
—Who wields a poem huger than the grave?
from only Whom shall time no refuge keep
though all the weird worlds must be opened?

)Love

here is the ocean,this is moonlight:say
that both precisely beyond either were—
so in darkness ourselves go,mind in mind

which is the thrilling least of all(for love's
secret supremely clothes herself with day)

i mean,should any curious dawn discuss
our mingling spirits,you would disappear
unreally;as this planet(understand)

forgets the entire and perpetual sea

—but if yourself consider wonderful
that your(how luminous)life toward twilight will
dissolve reintegrate beckon through me,
i think it is less wonderful than this

only by you my heart always moves

sonnet entitled how to run the world)

A always don't there B being no such thing
for C can't casts no shadow D drink and

E eat of her voice in whose silence the music of spring
lives F feel opens but shuts understand
G gladly forget little having less

with every least each most remembering
H highest fly only the flag that's furled

(sestet entitled grass is flesh or swim
who can and bathe who must or any dream
means more than sleep as more than know means guess)

I item i immaculately owe
dying one life and will my rest to these

children building this rainman out of snow

may i feel said he
(i'll squeal said she
just once said he)
it's fun said she

(may i touch said he
how much said she
a lot said he)
why not said she

(let's go said he
not too far said she
what's too far said he
where you are said she)

may i stay said he
(which way said she
like this said he
if you kiss said she

may i move said he
is it love said she)
if you're willing said he
(but you're killing said she

but it's life said he
but your wife said she
now said he)
ow said she

(tiptop said he
don't stop said she
oh no said he)
go slow said she

(cccome?said he
ummm said she)
you're divine!said he
(you are Mine said she)

he does not have to feel because he thinks
(the thoughts of others,be it understood)
he does not have to think because he knows
(that anything is bad which you think good)

because he knows,he cannot understand
(why Jones don't pay me what he knows he owes)
because he cannot understand,he drinks
(and he drinks and he drinks and he drinks and)

not bald.   (Coughs.)   Two pale slippery small eyes

balanced upon one broken babypout
(pretty teeth wander into which and out
of)Life,dost Thou contain a marvel than
this death named Smith less strange?
                              Married and lies

afraid;aggressive and:American

●

"let's start a magazine

to hell with literature
we want something redblooded

lousy with pure
reeking with stark
and fearlessly obscene

but really clean
get what I mean
let's not spoil it
let's make it serious

something authentic and delirious
you know something genuine like a mark
in a toilet

graced with guts and gutted
with grace"

squeeze your nuts and open your face

•

what does little Ernest croon
in his death at afternoon?
(kow dow r 2 bul retoinis
wus de woids uf lil Oinis

kumrads die because they're told)
kumrads die before they're old
(kumrads aren't afraid to die
kumrads don't
and kumrads won't
believe in life)and death knows whie

(all good kumrads you can tell
by their altruistic smell
moscow pipes good kumrads dance)
kumrads enjoy
s.freud knows whoy
the hope that you may mess your pance

every kumrad is a bit
of quite unmitigated hate
(travelling in a futile groove
god knows why)
and so do i
(because they are afraid to love

conceive a man,should he have anything
would give a little more than it away

(his autumn's winter being summer's spring
who moved by standing in november's may)
from whose(if loud most howish time derange

the silent whys of such a deathlessness)
remembrance might no patient mind unstrange
learn(nor could all earth's rotting scholars guess
that life shall not for living find the rule)

and dark beginnings are his luminous ends
who far less lonely than a fire is cool
took bedfellows for moons mountains for friends

—open your thighs to fate and(if you can
withholding nothing)World,conceive a man

●

at dusk
         just when
the Light is filled with birds
seriously
i begin

to climb the best hill,
driven by black wine.
a village does not move behind
my eye

the windmills are
silent
their flattened arms
complain steadily against the west

one Clock dimly cries
nine,i stride among the vines
(my heart pursues
against the little moon

a here and there lark
                    who;rises,
and;droops
as if upon a thread invisible)

A graveyard dreams through its
cluttered and brittle emblems,or
a field(and i pause among

the smell of minute mown lives)oh
my spirit you
tumble
climb
      and mightily fatally

i remark how through deep lifted
fields Oxen distinctly move,a
yellowandbluish cat(perched why
Curvingly at this)window;yes

women sturdily meander in my
mind,woven by always upon
sunset,
crickets within me whisper

whose erect blood finally
trembles,emerging to perceive
buried in cliff
           precisely

at the Ending of this road,
a candle in a shrine:
its puniest flame persists
shaken by the sea

Jehovah buried,Satan dead,
do fearers worship Much and Quick;
badness not being felt as bad,
itself thinks goodness what is meek;
obey says toc,submit says tic,
Eternity's a Five Year Plan:
if Joy with Pain shall hang in hock
who dares to call himself a man?

go dreamless knaves on Shadows fed,
your Harry's Tom, your Tom is Dick;
while Gadgets murder squawk and add,
the cult of Same is all the chic;
by instruments,both span and spic,
are justly measured Spic and Span:
to kiss the mike if Jew turn kike
who dares to call himself a man?

loudly for Truth have liars pled,
their heels for Freedom slaves will click;
where Boobs are holy,poets mad,
illustrious punks of Progress shriek;
when Souls are outlawed,Hearts are sick,
Hearts being sick,Minds nothing can:
if Hate's a game and Love's a φυκ
who dares to call himself a man?

King Christ,this world is all aleak;
and lifepreservers there are none:
and waves which only He may walk
Who dares to call Himself a man.

EPISODE TWO FROM *TOM*

the entire stagefloor is a drifting continuously pattern of irregularly squirming brightnesses: elsewhere lives black silence filled with perpetual falling of invisible snow

—spiralling out of high distant darkness, Eliza, with her doll clutched close, drops upon an inmost brightness

dance of Crossing The Icechoked River . . . Eliza
rising: totteringly balancing herself: on the squirming brightness, Eliza leapwhirls to another on which: staggering: she sinks; rises: balancingly: and whirlleaps to another—zigzagging gradually her way outward, toward the audience, from brightness to brightness
hither-and-thither meanwhile, in the high distant darkness from which Eliza came, spurt brutally luminous dogfaces; framing with intricate frustrations her crude whirlleaping-reelsinking-staggerrising-leapwhirling progress.
Precisely when, having almost gained the footlights, Eliza whirlleaps toward an outmost brightness—
the suddenly into itself shriveling lightriver becomes a mere twinkling thread across midstage; and
down out of dark distant height surging together bound dogmen
—between outpouring whom and her **a** curtain falls: halving the stage

light

Eliza has disappeared

the curtain satirizes a tavern interior; to lower left and right are painted groups of ferociously lolling lifesize carousers, facing the audience, with arms upraised and right hands clutching huge glasses. These drunkards have no faces

—vanitously enter, right-frontstage, a paragon of male elegance

dance of The Snob . . . George disguised
perfectly, at first, a vitality reduced to egotism imitates itself; artfully posturing, edits all categories of ostentation; generates, depthlessly gesturing, every species of insolent superciliousness. Gradually the linear meaning lessens, the danceplanes express themselves thickly; the puppet becomes a protagonist, the statue assumes manhood. Finally a man rips off a disguise—standing, bloody back to the audience, challenges two groups of painted spectators
—suddenly who wear the dogmasks of Haley's slave-catchers—

darkness

glowingly dogfaces vanish as the curtain rises on

Eliza (*), prostrate, her doll clutched to her heart:
in the high distant darkness behind and above Eliza, where luminous dogfaces spurted hither-and-thither, two lightdrenched figures appear. One, a mulatto woman (Cassy) resembling Eliza but taller and older, is leaning far backward with emaciated arms protectingly raised;

the other, a huge brutal white man (Legree), is towering over the woman with his right arm lifted and a black whip glittering in his right fist—
    slowly Cassy's backwardleaning body outwrithes, yearning toward her daughter
        —stumblingly Eliza rises; totterwhirlingly faces the apparation
            lightninglike, Legree's whip-fist-arm strikes: and the vision disappears

—halflight—

George, right-frontstage, whirlleaps inward, catching Eliza when she is about to fall—files of dogmen swoop from left- and right-midstage convergingly outward— enter, right- and left-backstage, a group of men and a group of women (the Friends or Quakers) all dressed in gray; all holding bibles over their hearts

outward swooping files of dogmen meet at the middle foreground—crisply advancing grey figures form a single line across the background in front of George and Eliza

inward surges a single file of dogmen—every Friend lowers his or her bible: and all the Quaker hearts glow with an unearthly radiance

—stopped, the column of attackers flattens itself from within outward; darkening, one after one, the dogmasks sink
    back, back a wilted terror cringes—step by crisp step
    a luminous phalanx marches toward the footlights
      —wildly to right and left fleeing Haley's slavecatchers disappear.

The inner wall of the stagecube opens, revealing a peaceful
landscape of sunlit mountains

dance of Thankfulness For Freedom . . . the Quakers,
George and Eliza covering their glowing hearts with
their bibles, bowed Friends kneel: George, clasping
Eliza, kneels also. Rising, the Friends turn crisply;
march erectly toward Eliza and George: rising and lifting slowly Eliza, George leapwhirls outward; halting,
back to the audience, at stagecentre. Crisply around
high her and erect him surging, the grey phalanx becomes a cross

    certainly a grey cross revolves:
    slowly the luminous Friends raise their bibles;
       proudly George lifts Eliza higher, highest
          slowly proudly Eliza lifts a child toward the
          mountains

BLACKOUT

●

(of Ever-Ever Land i speak
sweet morons gather roun'
who does not dare to stand or sit
may take it lying down)

down with the human soul
and anything else uncanned
for everyone carries canopeners
in Ever-Ever Land

(for Ever-Ever Land is a place
that's as simple as simple can be
and was built that way on purpose
by simple people like we)

down with hell and heaven
and all the religious fuss
infinity pleased our parents
one inch looks good to us

(and Ever-Ever Land is a place
that's measured and safe and known
where it's lucky to be unlucky
and the hitler lies down with the cohn)

down above all with love
and everything perverse
or which makes some feel more better
when all ought to feel less worse

(but only sameness is normal
in Ever-Ever Land
for a bad cigar is a woman
but a gland is only a gland)

this little bride & groom are
standing)in a kind
of crown he dressed
in black candy she

veiled with candy white
carrying a bouquet of
pretend flowers this
candy crown with this candy

little bride & little
groom in it kind of stands on
a thin ring which stands on a much
less thin very much more

big & kinder of ring & which
kinder of stands on a
much more than very much
biggest & thickest & kindest

of ring & all one two three rings
are cake & everything is protected by
cellophane against anything(because
nothing really exists

you shall above all things be glad and young.
For if you're young,whatever life you wear

it will become you;and if you are glad
whatever's living will yourself become.
Girlboys may nothing more than boygirls need:
i can entirely her only love

whose any mystery makes every man's
flesh put space on;and his mind take off time

that you should ever think,may god forbid
and(in his mercy)your true lover spare:
for that way knowledge lies,the foetal grave
called progress,and negation's dead undoom.

I'd rather learn from one bird how to sing
than teach ten thousand stars how not to dance

as freedom is a breakfastfood
or truth can live with right and wrong
or molehills are from mountains made
—long enough and just so long
will being pay the rent of seem
and genius please the talentgang
and water most encourage flame

as hatracks into peachtrees grow
or hopes dance best on bald men's hair
and every finger is a toe
and any courage is a fear
—long enough and just so long
will the impure think all things pure
and hornets wail by children stung

or as the seeing are the blind
and robins never welcome spring
nor flatfolk prove their world is round
nor dingsters die at break of dong
and common's rare and millstones float
—long enough and just so long
tomorrow will not be too late

worms are the words but joy's the voice
down shall go which and up come who
breasts will be breasts thighs will be thighs
deeds cannot dream what dreams can do
—time is a tree(this life one leaf)
but love is the sky and i am for you
just so long and long enough

buy me an ounce and i'll sell you a pound.
Turn
gert
    (spin!
helen)the
slimmer the finger the thicker the thumb(it's
whirl,
girls)
round and round

early to better is wiser for worse.
Give
liz
   (take!
tommy)we
order a steak and they send us a pie(it's
try,
boys)
mine is yours

ask me the name of the moon in the man.
Up
sam
    (down!
alice)a
hole in the ocean will never be missed(it's
in,
girls)
yours is mine

either was deafer than neither was dumb.
Skip
fred
   (jump!
neddy)but
under the wonder is over the why(it's
now,
boys)
here we come

●

there are possibly 2½ or impossibly 3
individuals every several fat
thousand years. Expecting more would be
neither fantastic nor pathological but

dumb. The number of times a wheel turns
doesn't determine its roundness:if swallows tryst
in your barn be glad;nobody ever earns
anything,everything little looks big in a mist

and if(by Him Whose blood was for us spilled)
than all mankind something more small occurs
or something more distorting than socalled
civilization i'll kiss a stalinist arse

in hitler's window on wednesday next at 1
E.S.T. bring the kiddies let's all have fun

anyone lived in a pretty how town
(with up so floating many bells down)
spring summer autumn winter
he sang his didn't he danced his did.

Women and men(both little and small)
cared for anyone not at all
they sowed their isn't they reaped their same
sun moon stars rain

children guessed(but only a few
and down they forgot as up they grew
autumn winter spring summer)
that noone loved him more by more

when by now and tree by leaf
she laughed his joy she cried his grief
bird by snow and stir by still
anyone's any was all to her

someones married their everyones
laughed their cryings and did their dance
(sleep wake hope and then)they
said their nevers they slept their dream

stars rain sun moon
(and only the snow can begin to explain
how children are apt to forget to remember
with up so floating many bells down)

one day anyone died i guess
(and noone stooped to kiss his face)
busy folk buried them side by side
little by little and was by was

all by all and deep by deep
and more by more they dream their sleep
noone and anyone earth by april
wish by spirit and if by yes.

Women and men(both dong and ding)
summer autumn winter spring
reaped their sowing and went their came
sun moon stars rain

my father moved through dooms of love
through sames of am through haves of give,
singing each morning out of each night
my father moved through depths of height

this motionless forgetful where
turned at his glance to shining here;
that if(so timid air is firm)
under his eyes would stir and squirm

newly as from unburied which
floats the first who,his april touch
drove sleeping selves to swarm their fates
woke dreamers to their ghostly roots

and should some why completely weep
my father's fingers brought her sleep:
vainly no smallest voice might cry
for he could feel the mountains grow.

Lifting the valleys of the sea
my father moved through griefs of joy;
praising a forehead called the moon
singing desire into begin

joy was his song and joy so pure
a heart of star by him could steer
and pure so now and now so yes
the wrists of twilight would rejoice

keen as midsummer's keen beyond
conceiving mind of sun will stand,
so strictly(over utmost him
so hugely)stood my father's dream

his flesh was flesh his blood was blood:
no hungry man but wished him food;
no cripple wouldn't creep one mile
uphill to only see him smile.

Scorning the pomp of must and shall
my father moved through dooms of feel;
his anger was as right as rain
his pity was as green as grain

septembering arms of year extend
less humbly wealth to foe and friend
than he to foolish and to wise
offered immeasurable is

proudly and(by octobering flame
beckoned)as earth will downward climb,
so naked for immortal work
his shoulders marched against the dark

his sorrow was as true as bread:
no liar looked him in the head;
if every friend became his foe
he'd laugh and build a world with snow.

My father moved through theys of we,
singing each new leaf out of each tree
(and every child was sure that spring
danced when she heard my father sing)

then let men kill which cannot share,
let blood and flesh be mud and mire,
scheming imagine,passion willed,
freedom a drug that's bought and sold

giving to steal and cruel kind,
a heart to fear,to doubt a mind,
to differ a disease of same,
conform the pinnacle of am

though dull were all we taste as bright,
bitter all utterly things sweet,
maggoty minus and dumb death
all we inherit,all bequeath

and nothing quite so least as truth
—i say though hate were why men breathe—
because my father lived his soul
love is the whole and more than all

of all the blessings which to man
kind progress doth impart
one stands supreme i mean the an
imal without a heart.

Huge this collective pseudobeast
(sans either pain or joy)
does nothing except preexist
its hoi in its polloi

and if sometimes he's prodded forth
to exercise her vote
(or made by threats of something worth
than death to change their coat

—which something as you'll never guess
in fifty thousand years
equals the quote and unquote loss
of liberty my dears—

or even is compelled to fight
itself from tame to teem)
still doth our hero contemplate
in raptures of undream

that strictly(and how)scienti
fic land of supernod
where freedom is compulsory
and only man is god.

Without a heart the animal
is very very kind
so kind it wouldn't like a soul
and couldn't use a mind

it was a goodly co
which paid to make man free
(for man is enslaved by a dread dizziz
and the sooner it's over the sooner to biz
don't ask me what it's pliz)

then up rose bishop budge from kew
a anglican was who
(with a rag and a bone and a hank of hair)'d
he picked up a thousand pounds or two
and he smote the monster merde

then up rose pride and up rose pelf
and ghibelline and guelph
and ladios and laddios
(on radios and raddios)
did save man from himself

ye duskiest despot's goldenest gal
did wring that dragon's tail
(for men must loaf and women must lay)
and she gave him a desdemonial
that took his breath away

all history oped her teeming womb
said demon for to doom
yea(fresh complexions being oke
with him)one william shakespeare broke
the silence of the tomb

then up rose mr lipshits pres
(who always nothing says)
and he kisséd the general menedjerr
and they smokéd a robert burns cigerr
to the god of things like they err

●

plato told

him:he couldn't
believe it(jesus

told him;he
wouldn't believe
it)lao

tsze
certainly told
him,and general
(yes

mam)
sherman;
and even
(believe it
or

not)you
told him:i told
him;we told him
(he didn't believe it,no

sir)it took
a nipponized bit of
the old sixth

avenue
el;in the top of his head:to tell

him

pity this busy monster,manunkind,

not.   Progress is a comfortable disease:
your victim(death and life safely beyond)

plays with the bigness of his littleness
—electrons deify one razorblade
into a mountainrange;lenses extend

unwish through curving wherewhen till unwish
returns on its unself.
                    A world of made
is not a world of born—pity poor flesh

and trees,poor stars and stones,but never this
fine specimen of hypermagical

ultraomnipotence.   We doctors know

a hopeless case if—listen:there's a hell
of a good universe next door;let's go

●

no man,if men are gods;but if gods must
be men,the sometimes only man is this
(most common,for each anguish is his grief;
and,for his joy is more than joy,most rare)

a fiend,if fiends speak truth;if angels burn

by their own generous completely light,
an angel;or(as various worlds he'll spurn
rather than fail immeasurable fate)
coward,clown,traitor,idiot,dreamer,beast—

such was a poet and shall be and is

—who'll solve the depths of horror to defend
a sunbeam's architecture with his life:
and carve immortal jungles of despair
to hold a mountain's heartbeat in his hand

old mr ly
fresh from a fu
ruddy as a sun
with blue true two

man
neral
rise
eyes

"this world's made 'bout
right it's the people that
abuses it you can git
anything you like out

of it if
you gut a mind
to there's something
for everybody it's a"

old mr lyman
ruddy as a sunrise
fresh with blue come
true from

a funeral
eyes
"big
thing"

all ignorance toboggans into know
and trudges up to ignorance again:
but winter's not forever,even snow
melts;and if spring should spoil the game,what then?

all history's a winter sport or three:
but were it five,i'd still insist that all
history is too small for even me;
for me and you,exceedingly too small.

Swoop(shrill collective myth)into thy grave
merely to toil the scale to shrillerness
per every madge and mabel dick and dave
—tomorrow is our permanent address

and there they'll scarcely find us(if they do,
we'll move away still further:into now

"sweet spring is your
time is my time is our
time for springtime is lovetime
and viva sweet love"

(all the merry little birds are
flying in the floating in the
very spirits singing in
are winging in the blossoming)

lovers go and lovers come
awandering awondering
but any two are perfectly
alone there's nobody else alive

(such a sky and such a sun
i never knew and neither did you
and everybody never breathed
quite so many kinds of yes)

not a tree can count his leaves
each herself by opening
but shining who by thousands mean
only one amazing thing

(secretly adoring shyly
tiny winging darting floating
merry in the blossoming
always joyful selves are singing)

"sweet spring is your
time is my time is our
time for springtime is lovetime
and viva sweet love"

when serpents bargain for the right to squirm
and the sun strikes to gain a living wage—
when thorns regard their roses with alarm
and rainbows are insured against old age

when every thrush may sing no new moon in
if all screech-owls have not okayed his voice
—and any wave signs on the dotted line
or else an ocean is compelled to close

when the oak begs permission of the birch
to make an acorn—valleys accuse their
mountains of having altitude—and march
denounces april as a saboteur

then we'll believe in that incredible
unanimal mankind(and not until)

who sharpens every dull
here comes the only man
reminding with his bell
to disappear a sun

and out of houses pour
maids mothers widows wives
bringing this visitor
their very oldest lives

one pays him with a smile
another with a tear
some cannot pay at all
he never seems to care

he sharpens is to am
he sharpens say to sing
you'd almost cut your thumb
so right he sharpens wrong

and when their lives are keen
he throws the world a kiss
and slings his wheel upon
his back and off he goes

but we can hear him still
if now our sun is gone
reminding with his bell
to reappear a moon

honour corruption villainy holiness
riding in fragrance of sunlight(side by side
all in a singing wonder of blossoming yes
riding)to him who died that death should be dead

humblest and proudest eagerly wandering
(equally all alive in miraculous day)
merrily moving through sweet forgiveness of spring
(over the under the gift of the earth of the sky

knight and ploughman pardoner wife and nun
merchant frere clerk somnour miller and reve
and geoffrey and all)come up from the never of when
come into the now of forever come riding alive

down while crylessly drifting through vast most
nothing's own nothing children go of dust

the great advantage of being alive
(instead of undying)is not so much
that mind no more can disprove than prove
what heart may feel and soul may touch
—the great(my darling)happens to be
that love are in we,that love are in we

and here is a secret they never will share
for whom create is less than have
or one times one than when times where—
that we are in love,that we are in love:
with us they've nothing times nothing to do
(for love are in we am in i are in you)

this world(as timorous itsters all
to call their cowardice quite agree)
shall never discover our touch and feel
—for love are in we are in love are in we;
for you are and i am and we are(above
and under all possible worlds)in love

a billion brains may coax undeath
from fancied fact and spaceful time—
no heart can leap,no soul can breathe
but by the sizeless truth of a dream
whose sleep is the sky and the earth and the sea.
For love are in you am in i are in we

when faces called flowers float out of the ground
and breathing is wishing and wishing is having—
but keeping is downward and doubting and never
—it's april(yes,april;my darling)it's spring!
yes the pretty birds frolic as spry as can fly
yes the little fish gambol as glad as can be
(yes the mountains are dancing together)

when every leaf opens without any sound
and wishing is having and having is giving—
but keeping is doting and nothing and nonsense
—alive;we're alive,dear:it's(kiss me now)spring!
now the pretty birds hover so she and so he
now the little fish quiver so you and so i
(now the mountains are dancing,the mountains)

when more than was lost has been found has been found
and having is giving and giving is living—
but keeping is darkness and winter and cringing
—it's spring(all our night becomes day)o,it's spring!
all the pretty birds dive to the heart of the sky
all the little fish climb through the mind of the sea
(all the mountains are dancing;are dancing)

●

now all the fingers of this tree(darling)have
hands,and all the hands have people;and
more each particular person is(my love)
alive than every world can understand

and now you are and i am now and we're
a mystery which will never happen again,
a miracle which has never happened before—
and shining this our now must come to then

our then shall be some darkness during which
fingers are without hands;and i have no
you:and all trees are(any more than each
leafless)its silent in forevering snow

—but never fear(my own,my beautiful
my blossoming)for also then's until

crazy jay blue)
demon laughshriek
ing at me
your scorn of easily

hatred of timid
& loathing for(dull all
regular righteous
comfortable)unworlds

thief crook cynic
(swimfloatdrifting
fragment of heaven)
trickstervillain

raucous rogue &
vivid voltaire
you beautiful anarchist
(i salute thee

maggie and milly and molly and may
went down to the beach(to play one day)

and maggie discovered a shell that sang
so sweetly she couldn't remember her troubles,and

milly befriended a stranded star
whose rays five languid fingers were;

and molly was chased by a horrible thing
which raced sideways while blowing bubbles:and

may came home with a smooth round stone
as small as a world and as large as alone.

For whatever we lose(like a you or a me)
it's always ourselves we find in the sea

lily has a rose
(i have none)
"don't cry dear violet
you may take mine"

"o how how how
could i ever wear it now
when the boy who gave it to
you is the tallest of the boys"

"he'll give me another
if i let him kiss me twice
but my lover has a brother
who is good and kind to all"

"o no no no
let the roses come and go
for kindness and goodness do
not make a fellow tall"

lily has a rose
no rose i've
and losing's less than winning(but
love is more than love)

in time of daffodils(who know
the goal of living is to grow)
forgetting why,remember how

in time of lilacs who proclaim
the aim of waking is to dream,
remember so(forgetting seem)

in time of roses(who amaze
our now and here with paradise)
forgetting if,remember yes

in time of all sweet things beyond
whatever mind may comprehend,
remember seek(forgetting find)

and in a mystery to be
(when time from time shall set us free)
forgetting me,remember me

●

once White&Gold

daisy in the Dust
(trite now and old)

lie we so must

most lily brief

(rose here&gone)
flesh all is If

all blood And When

●

albutnotquitemost

lost(in this br
am
bliest tangle of hi
llside)a

few dim tombstones

try to re(still u
ntumbled but slant
ing drun
kenly)mind

me of noone i ever &

someone(the others have
long ago laid
them)i never(selves
any than

every more silent

ly)heard(& how
look at it blue is the
high is
the deep is the far o my

darling)of(down

●

that melancholy

fellow'll play
his handorgan
until you say

"i want a fortune"

.At which(smiling)he stops:
& pick
ing up a magical stick
t,a,p,s

this dingy cage:then with a ghost

's rainfaint windthin
voice-which-is
no-voice sobcries

"paw?lee"

—whereupon out(SlO
wLy)steps(to
mount the wand)a by no
means almost

white morethanPerson;who

(riding through space
to diminutive this
opened drawer)tweak

S with his brutebeak

one fatal faded(pinkish or
yellowish maybe)piece
of pitiful paper—
but now, as Mr bowing Cockatoo

proffers the meaning of the stars

14th st dis(because my tears
are full of eyes)appears. Because
only the truest things always

are true because they can't be true

"so you're hunting for ann well i'm looking for will"
"did you look for him down by the old swimminghole"
"i'd be worse than a fool to have never looked there"
"and you couldn't well miss willy's carroty hair"

"it seems like i just heard your annabel screech
have you hunted her round by the rasberrypatch"
"i have hunted her low i have hunted her high
and that pretty pink pinafore'd knock out your eye"

"well maybe she's up to some tricks with my bill
as long as there's haymows you never can tell"
"as long as there's ladies my annie is one
nor she wouldn't be seen with the likes of your son"

"and who but your daughter i'm asking yes who
but that sly little bitch could have showed billy how"
"your bastard boy must have learned what he knows
from his slut of a mother i rather suppose"

"will's dad never gave me one cent in his life
but he fell for a whore when he married his wife
and here is a riddle for you red says
it aint his daughter her father lays"

"black hell upon you and all filthy men
come annabel darling come annie come ann"
"she's coming right now in the rasberrypatch
and 'twas me that she asked would it hurt too much

and 'twas me that looked up at my willy and you
in the newmown hay and he telling you no"
"then look you down through the old swimminghole
there'll be slime in his eyes and a stone on his soul"

●

from spiralling ecstatically this

proud nowhere of earth's most prodigious night
blossoms a newborn babe:around him,eyes
—gifted with every keener appetite
than mere unmiracle can quite appease—
humbly in their imagined bodies kneel
(over time space doom dream while floats the whole

perhapsless mystery of paradise)

mind without soul may blast some universe
to might have been,and stop ten thousand stars
but not one heartbeat of this child;nor shall
even prevail a million questionings
against the silence of his mother's smile

—whose only secret all creation sings

—laughing to find
anyone's blind
(like me like you)
except in snow—

a whom we make
(of grin for smile
whose head's his face
with stones for eyes

for mind with none)
boy after girl
each brings a world
to build our clown

—shouting to see
what no mind knows
a mindless he
begins to guess

what no tongue tells
(such as ourselves)
begins to sing
an only grin—

dancing to feel
nots are their whys
stones become eyes
locks open keys

haven't is have
doubt and believe
(like me like you)
vanish in so

—laughing to find
a noone's more
by far than you're
alive or i'm—

crying to lose
(as down someone
who's we ungrows)
a dream in the rain

●

why

do the
fingers

of the lit
tle once beau
tiful la

dy(sitting sew
ing at an o
pen window this
fine morning)fly

instead of dancing
are they possibly
afraid that life is
running away from
them(i wonder)or

isn't she a
ware that life(who
never grows old)
is always beau

tiful and
that nobod
y beauti

ful ev
er hur

ries

home means that
when the certainly
roof leaks it
's our(home

means if any moon
or possibly
sun shines they are
our also my

darling)but should some im
probably
unworld crash
to 1

nonillion(& so)nothings
each(let's
kiss)means
home

old age sticks
up Keep
Off
signs)&

youth yanks them
down(old
age
cries No

Tres)&(pas)
youth laughs
(sing
old age

scolds Forbid
den Stop
Must
n't Don't

&)youth goes
right on
gr
owing old

a total stranger one black day
knocked living the hell out of me—

who found forgiveness hard because
my(as it happened)self he was

—but now that fiend and i are such
immortal friends the other's each

●

stand with your lover on the ending earth—

and while a(huge which by which huger than
huge)whoing sea leaps to greenly hurl snow

suppose we could not love,dear;imagine

ourselves like living neither nor dead these
(or many thousand hearts which don't and dream
or many million minds which sleep and move)
blind sands,at pitiless the mercy of

time time time time time

—how fortunate are you and i,whose home
is timelessness:we who have wandered down
from fragrant mountains of eternal now

to frolic in such mysteries as birth
and death a day(or maybe even less)

●

i shall imagine life
is not worth dying,if
(and when)roses complain
their beauties are in vain

but though mankind persuades
itself that every weed's
a rose,roses(you feel
certain)will only smile

i am a little church(no great cathedral)
far from the splendor and squalor of hurrying cities
—i do not worry if briefer days grow briefest,
i am not sorry when sun and rain make april

my life is the life of the reaper and the sower;
my prayers are prayers of earth's own clumsily striving
(finding and losing and laughing and crying)children
whose any sadness or joy is my grief or my gladness

around me surges a miracle of unceasing
birth and glory and death and resurrection:
over my sleeping self float flaming symbols
of hope,and i wake to a perfect patience of mountains

i am a little church(far from the frantic
world with its rapture and anguish)at peace with nature
—i do not worry if longer nights grow longest;
i am not sorry when silence becomes singing

winter by spring,i lift my diminutive spire to
merciful Him Whose only now is forever:
standing erect in the deathless truth of His presence
(welcoming humbly His light and proudly His darkness)

unlove's the heavenless hell and homeless home

of knowledgeable shadows(quick to seize
each nothing which all soulless wraiths proclaim
substance;all heartless spectres,happiness)

lovers alone wear sunlight. The whole truth

not hid by matter;not by mind revealed
(more than all dying life,all living death)
and never which has been or will be told

sings only—and all lovers are the song.

Here(only here)is freedom :always here
no then of winter equals now of spring;
but april's day transcends november's year

(eternity being so sans until
twice i have lived forever in a smile)

i carry your heart with me(i carry it in
my heart)i am never without it(anywhere
i go you go,my dear;and whatever is done
by only me is your doing,my darling)
                                    i fear
no fate(for you are my fate,my sweet)i want
no world(for beautiful you are my world,my true)
and it's you are whatever a moon has always meant
and whatever a sun will always sing is you

here is the deepest secret nobody knows
(here is the root of the root and the bud of the bud
and the sky of the sky of a tree called life;which grows
higher than soul can hope or mind can hide)
and this is the wonder that's keeping the stars apart

i carry your heart(i carry it in my heart)

spring!may—
everywhere's here
(with a low high low
and the bird on the bough)
how?why
—we never we know
(so kiss me)shy sweet eagerly my
most dear

(die!live)
the new is the true
and to lose is to have
—we never we know—
brave!brave
(the earth and the sky
are one today)my very so gay
young love

why?how—
we never we know
(with a high low high
in the may in the spring)
live!die
(forever is now)
and dance you suddenly blossoming tree
—i'll sing

being to timelessness as it's to time,
love did no more begin than love will end;
where nothing is to breathe to stroll to swim
love is the air the ocean and the land

(do lovers suffer?all divinities
proudly descending put on deathful flesh:
are lovers glad?only their smallest joy's
a universe emerging from a wish)

love is the voice under all silences,
the hope which has no opposite in fear;
the strength so strong mere force is feebleness:
the truth more first than sun more last than star

—do lovers love?why then to heaven with hell.
Whatever sages say and fools,all's well

if up's the word;and a world grows greener
minute by second and most by more—
if death is the loser and life is the winner
(and beggars are rich but misers are poor)
—let's touch the sky:

                with a to and a fro
(and a here there where)and away we go

in even the laziest creature among us
a wisdom no knowledge can kill is astir—
now dull eyes are keen and now keen eyes are keener
(for young is the year,for young is the year)
—let's touch the sky:

                with a great(and a gay
and a steep)deep rush through amazing day

it's brains without hearts have set saint against sinner;
put gain over gladness and joy under care—
let's do as an earth which can never do wrong does
(minute by second and most by more)
—let's touch the sky:

                with a strange(and a true)
and a climbing fall into far near blue

if beggars are rich(and a robin will sing his
robin a song)but misers are poor—
let's love until noone could quite be(and young is
the year,dear)as living as i'm and as you're
—let's touch the sky:

                with a you and a me
and an every(who's any who's some)one who's we

●

O the sun comes up-up-up in the opening

sky(the all the
any merry every pretty each

bird sings birds sing
gay-be-gay because today's today)the
romp cries i and the me purrs

you and the gentle
who-horns says-does moo-woo
(the prance with the
three white its stimpstamps)

the grintgrunt wugglewiggle
champychumpchomps yes
the speckled strut begins to scretch and
scratch-scrutch

and scritch(while
the no-she-yes-he fluffies tittle
tattle did-he-does-she)& the

ree ray rye roh
rowster shouts

rawrOO

for any ruffian of the sky
your kingbird doesn't give a damn—
his royal warcry is I AM
and he's the soul of chivalry

in terror of whose furious beak
(as sweetly singing creatures know)
cringes the hugest heartless hawk
and veers the vast most crafty crow

your kingbird doesn't give a damn
for murderers of high estate
whose mongrel creed is Might Makes Right
—his royal warcry is I AM

true to his mate his chicks his friends
he loves because he cannot fear
(you see it in the way he stands
and looks and leaps upon the air)

●

seeker of truth

follow no path
all paths lead where

truth is here

●

SONG

but we've the may
(for you are in love
and i am)to sing,
my darling:while
old worlds and young
(big little and all
worlds)merely have
the must to say

and the when to do
is exactly theirs
(dull worlds or keen;
big little and all)
but lose or win
(come heaven,come hell)
precisely ours
is the now to grow

it's love by whom
(my beautiful friend)
the gift to live
is without until:
but pitiful they've
(big little and all)
no power beyond
the trick to seem

their joys turn woes
and right goes wrong
(dim worlds or bright;
big little and all)
whereas(my sweet)

our summer in fall
and in winter our spring
is the yes of yes

love was and shall
be this only truth
(a dream of a deed,
born not to die)
but worlds are made
of hello and goodbye:
glad sorry or both
(big little and all)

●

the first of all my dreams was of
a lover and his only love,
strolling slowly(mind in mind)
through some green mysterious land

until my second dream begins—
the sky is wild with leaves;which dance
and dancing swoop(and swooping whirl
over a frightened boy and girl)

but that mere fury soon became
silence:in huger always whom
two tiny selves sleep(doll by doll)
motionless under magical

foreverfully falling snow.
And then this dreamer wept:and so
she quickly dreamed a dream of spring
—how you and i are blossoming

●

fair ladies tall lovers
riding are through the
(with wonder into colours
all into singing)may

wonder a with deep
(A so wonder pure)
even than the green
the new the earth more

moving(all gay
fair brave tall young
come they)through the may
in fragrance and song

wonderingly come
(brighter than prayers)
riding through a Dream
like fire called flowers

over green the new
earth a day of may
under more a blue
than blue can be sky

always(through fragrance
and singing)come lovers
with slender their ladies
(Each youngest)in sunlight

●

everybody happy?
WE-WE-WE
& to hell with the chappy
who doesn't agree

(if you can't dentham
comma bentham;
or 1 law for the lions &
oxen is science)

Q:how numb can an unworld get?
A:number

●

why

don't
be
sil
ly

,o no in-

deed;
money
can't do(never
did &

never will)any

damn
thing
:far
from it;you

're wrong,my friend. But

what does
do,
has always done
;&

will do alw

-ays something
is(guess)yes
you're
right:my enemy

.   Love

●

nite)
thatthis
crou
    ched

moangrowl-&-thin
g stirs(m
id)a
life whats wh

(un)ich(cur
ling)s
    ilentl
y are(mi

dnite also conce
als 2 ph
antoms clutch
ed in

a writhewho room)as
hows of
whi
    ne
        climbscr

e
AM
e
xploding aRe(n't

●

a grin without a
face(a look
without an i)
be care

ful(touch noth
ing)or
it'll disapp
ear bangl

essly(into sweet
the earth)&
nobody
(including our

selves)
will reme
mber
(for 1 frac

tion of
a mo
ment)where
what how

when
who why
which
(or anything)

if seventy were young
and death uncommon
(forgiving not divine,
to err inhuman)
or any thine a mine
—dingdong :dongding—
to say would be to sing

if broken hearts were whole
and cowards heroes
(the popular the wise,
a weed a tearose)
and every minus plus
—fare ill :fare well—
a frown would be a smile

if sorrowful were gay
(today tomorrow,
doubting believing and
to lend to borrow)
or any foe a friend
—cry nay :cry yea—
november would be may

that you and i'd be quite
—come such perfection—
another i and you,
is a deduction
which(be it false or true)
disposes me to shoot
dogooding folk on sight

in heavenly realms of hellas dwelt
two very different sons of zeus:
one,handsome strong and born to dare
—a fighter to his eyelashes—
the other,cunning ugly lame;
but as you'll shortly comprehend
a marvellous artificer

now Ugly was the husband of
(as happens every now and then
upon a merely human plane)
someone completely beautiful;
and Beautiful,who(truth to sing)
could never quite tell right from wrong,
took brother Fearless by the eyes
and did the deed of joy with him

then Cunning forged a web so subtle
air is comparatively crude;
an indestructible occult
supersnare of resistless metal:
and(stealing toward the blissful pair)
skilfully wafted over themselves this implacable unthing

next,our illustrious scientist
petitions the celestial host
to scrutinize his handiwork:
they(summoned by that savage yell
from shining realms of regions dark)
laugh long at Beautiful and Brave
—wildly who rage,vainly who strive;
and being finally released
flee one another like the pest

thus did immortal jealousy
quell divine generosity,
thus reason vanquished instinct and
matter became the slave of mind;
thus virtue triumphed over vice
and beauty bowed to ugliness
and logic thwarted life:and thus—
but look around you,friends and foes

my tragic tale concludes herewith:
soldier,beware of mrs smith

the greedy the people
(as if as can yes)
they sell and they buy
and they die for because
though the bell in the steeple
says Why

the chary the wary
(as all as can each)
they don't and they do
and they turn to a which
though the moon in her glory
says Who

the busy the millions
(as you're as can i'm)
they flock and they flee
through a thunder of seem
though the stars in their silence
say Be

the cunning the craven
(as think as can feel)
they when and they how
and they live for until
though the sun in his heaven
says Now

the timid the tender
(as doubt as can trust)
they work and they pray
and they bow to a must
though the earth in her splendor
says May

one winter afternoon

(at the magical hour
when is becomes if)

a bespangled clown
standing on eighth street
handed me a flower.

Nobody,it's safe,
to say,observed him but

myself;and why?because

without any doubt he was
whatever(first and last)

mostpeople fear most:
a mystery for which i've
no word except alive

—that is,completely alert
and miraculously whole;

with not merely a mind and a heart

but unquestionably a soul—
by no means funereally hilarious

(or otherwise democratic)
but essentially poetic
or ethereally serious:

a fine not a coarse clown
(no mob,but a person)

and while never saying a word

who was anything but dumb;
since the silence of him

self sang like a bird.
Mostpeople have been heard
screaming for international

measures that render hell rational
—i thank heaven somebody's crazy

enough to give me a daisy

if in beginning twilight of winter will stand

(over a snowstopped silent world)one
spirit serenely truly himself;and

alone only as greatness is alone—

one(above nevermoving all nowhere)
goldenly whole,prodigiously alive
most mercifully glorying keen star

whom she-and-he-like ifs of am perceive

(but believe scarcely may)certainly while
mute each inch of their murdered planet grows
more and enormously more less:until
her-and-his nonexistence vanishes

with also earth's
                    —"dying" the ghost of you
whispers "is very pleasant" my ghost to

white guardians of the universe of sleep

safely may by imperishable your
glory escorted through infinite countries be
my darling(open the very secret of hope
to her eyes,not any longer blinded with
a world;and let her heart's each whisper wear

all never guessed unknowable most joy)

faithfully blossoming beyond to breathe
suns of the night,bring this beautiful
wanderer home to a dream called time:and give
herself into the mercy of that star,
if out of climbing whom begins to spill
such golden blood as makes his moon alive

sing more will wonderfully birds than are

●

your homecoming will be my homecoming—

my selves go with you,only i remain;
a shadow phantom effigy or seeming

(an almost someone always who's noone)

a noone who,till their and your returning,
spends the forever of his loneliness
dreaming their eyes have opened to your morning

feeling their stars have risen through your skies:

so,in how merciful love's own name,linger
no more than selfless i can quite endure
the absence of that moment when a stranger
takes in his arms my very life who's your

—when all fears hopes beliefs doubts disappear.
Everywhere and joy's perfect wholeness we're

a round face near the top of the stairs
speaks in his kind sweet big voice:
then a slender face(on the mantlepiece
of a bedroom)begins to croon

more particularly at just
midnight this hearty fellow'll exist
—whereas that delicate creature is most
herself while uttering one

a third face,away in the sky
finally faintly(higher than high
in the rain in the wind in the dark)whispers.
And i and my love are alone

Now i lay(with everywhere around)
me(the great dim deep sound
of rain;and of always and of nowhere)and

what a gently welcoming darkestness—

now i lay me down(in a most steep
more than music)feeling that sunlight is
(life and day are)only loaned:whereas
night is given(night and death and the rain

are given;and given is how beautifully snow)

now i lay me down to dream of(nothing
i or any somebody or you
can begin to begin to imagine)

something which nobody may keep.
now i lay me down to dream of Spring

●

without the mercy of
your eyes your
voice your
ways(o very most my shining love)

how more than dark i am,
no song(no
thing)no
silence ever told;it has no name—

but should this namelessness
(completely
fleetly)
vanish,at the infinite precise

thrill of your beauty,then
my lost my
dazed my
whereful selves they put on here again

—to livingest one star
as small these
all these
thankful(hark)birds singing wholly are

faithfully tinying at twilight voice
of deathless earth's innumerable doom:
againing(yes by microscopic yes)
acceptance of irrevocable time

particular pure truth of patience heard
above the everywhereing fact of fear;
and under any silence of each bird
who dares to not forsake a failing year

—now,before quite your whisper's whisper is
subtracted from my hope's own hope,receive
(undaunted guest of dark most downwardness
and marvellously self diminutive

whose universe a single leaf may be)
the more than thanks of always merest me

who are you,little i

(five or six years old)
peering from some high

window;at the gold

of november sunset

(and feeling:that if day
has to become night

this is a beautiful way)

now does our world descend
the path to nothingness
(cruel now cancels kind;
friends turn to enemies)
therefore lament,my dream
and don a doer's doom

create is now contrive;
imagined,merely know
(freedom:what makes a slave)
therefore,my life,lie down
and more by most endure
all that you never were

hide,poor dishonoured mind
who thought yourself so wise;
and much could understand
concerning no and yes:
if they've become the same
it's time you unbecame

where climbing was and bright
is darkness and to fall
(now wrong's the only right
since brave are cowards all)
therefore despair,my heart
and die into the dirt

but from this endless end
of briefer each our bliss—
where seeing eyes go blind
(where lips forget to kiss)
where everything's nothing
—arise,my soul;and sing

"o purple finch

           please tell me why
this summer world(and you and i
who love so much to live)

                must die"

"if i

      should tell you anything"
(that eagerly sweet carolling
self answers me)

           "i could not sing"

how many moments must(amazing each
how many centuries)these more than eyes
restroll and stroll some never deepening beach

locked in foreverish time's tide at poise,

love alone understands:only for whom
i'll keep my tryst until that tide shall turn;
and from all selfsubstracting hugely doom
treasures of reeking innocence are born.

Then,with not credible the anywhere
eclipsing of a spirit's ignorance
by every wisdom knowledge fears to dare,

how the(myself's own self who's)child will dance!

and when he's plucked such mysteries as men
do not conceive—let ocean grow again

all worlds have halfsight,seeing either with

life's eye(which is if things seem spirits)or
(if spirits in the guise of things appear)
death's:any world must always half perceive.

Only whose vision can create the whole

(being forever born a foolishwise
proudhumble citizen of ecstasies
more steep than climb can time with all his years)

he's free into the beauty of the truth;

and strolls the axis of the universe
—love. Each believing world denies,whereas
your lover(looking through both life and death)
timelessly celebrates the merciful

wonder no world deny may or believe

INDEX OF FIRST LINES

190